Routledge Revivals

Karl Marx

Achille Loria was a well-known Italian political economist and this translation of his work presents his views and discussions on famous socialist Karl Marx, bringing his work to an English audience. Originally published in 1917, the translators have included a detailed foreword which attempts to put Loria's work in context of other views on Marxism. This title will be of interest to students of politics and sociology.

Karl Marx

Achille Loria
Translated by
Eden & Cedar Paul

First published in 1920
by George Allen & Unwin Ltd

This edition first published in 2016 by Routledge
2 Park Square, Milton Park, Abingdon, Oxon, OX14 4RN
and by Routledge
711 Third Avenue, New York, NY 10017

Routledge is an imprint of the Taylor & Francis Group, an informa business

© 1920 Eden & Cedar Paul

All rights reserved. No part of this book may be reprinted or reproduced or utilised in any form or by any electronic, mechanical, or other means, now known or hereafter invented, including photocopying and recording, or in any information storage or retrieval system, without permission in writing from the publishers.

Publisher's Note
The publisher has gone to great lengths to ensure the quality of this reprint but points out that some imperfections in the original copies may be apparent.

Disclaimer
The publisher has made every effort to trace copyright holders and welcomes correspondence from those they have been unable to contact.

A Library of Congress record exists under LC control number: 20014209

ISBN 13: 978-1-138-64046-7 (hbk)
ISBN 13: 978-1-315-63656-6 (ebk)
ISBN 13: 978-1-138-64051-1 (pbk)

KARL MARX

BY

ACHILLE LORIA

AUTHORISED TRANSLATION FROM THE ITALIAN
WITH A FOREWORD

BY

EDEN & CEDAR PAUL

LONDON: GEORGE ALLEN & UNWIN LTD.
RUSKIN HOUSE, 40 MUSEUM STREET, W.C. 1

First published in 1920

(All rights reserved)

The socialism that inspires hopes and fears to-day is of the school of Marx. No one is seriously apprehensive of any other so-called socialistic movement, and no one is seriously concerned to criticise or refute the doctrines set forth by any other school of " socialists.

FOREWORD
BY
EDEN AND CEDAR PAUL

FOREWORD

IT has been said that the professional and professorial exponents of economic science confine themselves to variants of a single theme. Usually belonging to the master class by birth and education, and at any rate attached to that class by the ties of economic interest, they are ever guided by the conscious or subconscious aim of providing a theoretical justification for the capitalist system, and their lives are devoted to inculcating the art of extracting honey from the hive without alarming the bees. Achille Loria is an exception to this generalisation. Professor of political economy at Turin, and one of the most learned economists of the day, he is anything but an apologist for the bourgeois economy. With the exception of the first volume of Marx's *Capital*, no more telling indictment of capitalism has ever been penned than Loria's *Analysis of Capitalist Property* (1889). This gigantic work has not been translated, but a number of Loria's books are available to English readers: *The Economic Foundations of Society*, 1902; *Contemporary Social Problems*, 1911; *The Economic Synthesis*, 1914. A biographical and critical study of Malthus, in the Italian an early volume of the series of booklets of which the present essay on Marx forms one of the latest issues, was rendered into English in 1917 and published in the United States as the opening chapter of a symposium on *Population and Birth Control*

KARL MARX

edited by the writers of this foreword. *The Economic Foundations of Society* has run through five editions in Swan Sonnenschein's (now Allen & Unwin's) "Social Science Series." But on the whole Loria's works are less widely known in England than on the continent, far less widely known than they deserve to be. An exposition of his outlook and a study of his relationship to Marx will not only be of interest in themselves, but will help readers to surmount certain terminological difficulties in the *Karl Marx*. All original thinkers write perforce in a language of their own minting. Those of us to whom "surplus value," the "class struggle," the "materialist conception," "economic determinism," have been familiar concepts from childhood upwards, are apt to forget that Marx's contemporaries were repelled by what they regarded as superfluous jargon. The first students of Kant, the first students of Darwin, the first students of all great innovators in philosophy, science, and the arts, have had to master a new vocabulary before they could understand what these writers were driving at; for new ideas must be conveyed in a new speech or by the use of old words refashioned. We cannot understand Loria, we cannot appreciate Loria's criticism of Marx, we cannot grasp the nature of Loria's own affiliation to Marx, unless we realise precisely what the Italian economist means by the speciously familiar terms "income," "subsistence," "unproductive labourers," "recipients of income," and the like. The familiarity of the words makes them all the more misleading to those who do not hold the Lorian clue to guide them through the economic labyrinth. Does this sound alarming? Yet Loria's doctrines, like those of Marx, like those of Darwin, like those of — but we must not say "like those of Kant"—are simplicity

FOREWORD

itself to anyone who is able to survive the first shock of the encounter, to surmount the first agony of a new idea.

In our own view the difficulty of economics in large part depends upon the fact that it is either a system of apologetics or else a system of attack. There are, in fact, two conflicting sciences: the economic science of the master class, and the economic science of the proletariat. Both are necessarily tendentious, and the conflicting tendencies will remain irreconcilable as long as the class struggle continues. Not until that struggle has been fought to a successful issue, not until the co-operative commonwealth has come into existence, can there be a comparatively dispassionate political economy. As dispassionate as conic sections it can never be, for it is biological, sociological, is by its very nature tinged with human interest, and can therefore never be wholly impartial. But many of the contradictions and perplexities of economics are by no means inherent; they are, we contend, no more than confusing reflexes of the class struggle. Loria seems to hold a somewhat similar opinion. In *Contemporary Social Problems* (pp. 99, 100) he writes: " I am inclined to consider political economy and socialism as two intellectual weapons which, for a long time separate and mutually antagonistic owing to the apologetic theories of the one and the subversive utopianism of the other, are drawing closer and closer together as they become more human and the old animosities disappear. Perhaps the day is not far distant when the two forces will unite under one standard." To a casual reader this might suggest that Loria thinks that the class struggle, that the conflict between orthodox economics and socialism, can be overcome within the framework of the bourgeois economy

—that the capitalist Old-Man-of-the-Sea can at one and the same time remain seated upon the back of the proletarian Sindbad the Sailor, and walk beside him amicably arm in arm as the two climb the mount of human endeavour. But an attentive student of Loria's *Karl Marx* will realise that when the Italian speaks of "a day not far distant," he means the morrow of the social revolution, when Marx's promethean work shall have been completed, and when, led by Marx "the emperor in the realm of mind," the human race shall have reached "the brilliant goal which awaits it in a future not perhaps immeasurably remote" (infra p. 91).

For Loria, one of the greatest living champions of the doctrine of economic determinism, sees no difficulty in reconciling that doctrine with a firm belief in the magistral efficacy, at the stage which evolution has now reached, of the deliberate human will. "The economic natural force," writes Eduard Bernstein (*Evolutionary Socialism*, p. 14), "like the physical, changes from the ruler of mankind to its servant, according as its nature is recognised." Herein is embodied the application in the special economic field of the profound general truth that by scientific study man, the child of nature, learns to control nature, and thereby to mould his own being and social environment in accordance with the dictates of his own enlightened will. Similarly Loria is far from the rigid economic determinism which would refuse to admit the existence of "ideal" causation, or the possibility in the sphere of sociology of intelligently adapting means to ends. "Idealism" is a word which has been soiled by such ignoble use that one really hesitates to employ it; but we must distinguish between idealism and sentimentalism, and between idealism and window dressing. The right sort of idealism is realist

FOREWORD

idealism, and Loria is a realist idealist. He distinguishes clearly between fatalism and quietism, on the one hand, and economic determinism tempered by rationalist guidance, on the other. In *The Economic Foundations of Society* (pp. 376 et seq.) he writes: " Can we say that a doctrine leads to fatalism which concedes a fertile field to human activity, and which only seeks to mark out the limits within which such efforts may be applied ? Can we give the name of quietism to a theory whose aims lie in the direction of substituting enlightened action aware of its ends, for blind and ignorant innovation which is powerless to realise its purposes ? . . . Turning to consider the great social transformations which alter the structure of property, our theory does, it is true, deny that such movements can be effected before the necessary change in economic conditions has rendered them inevitable ; but far from this conclusion leading to the degradation of human nature, it seems to us to inspire the highest sentiments. If we examine the great spontaneous movements that have sought to modify economic conditions before their time, we shall find that they all lacked definite purpose. There was no clear idea of the new order of things to be substituted for the old ; on this account these movements were wanting in discipline ; they were anarchic, and hence their lack of effect. Our theory, on the contrary, declares that it is first of all necessary to learn the nature of the future social system, and, after this knowledge has been acquired, to substitute a co-ordination of effort towards this rigorously determined end for the blind and disorganised attempts that have thus far been made in this direction. . . . Far from leading towards fatalism our theory tends to encourage rational human activity, which alone can prevent, or at least mitigate, the confusion otherwise attendant upon the social metamorphosis. . . . A wide field is thus opened to human activity, and it is certainly a noble mission for mankind to withdraw social development from the operation of the blind and brutal forces of physical evolution, and to submit the process to the kindlier and more civilised action of human reason."

The definitive exposition of Loria's views is to be found in *The Economic Synthesis*; but since in his theory of social evolution the effects of increasing population play so notable a part, reference must first be made to his examination of Malthus' theory of population. At the outset, however, let us recall Marx's attitude to the Malthusian doctrine. Marx rejected the idea that, for human beings, population tends to grow in such a manner as necessarily to press on the means of subsistence. Though he accepted Darwinism and had a profound admiration for Darwin, as far as the human species is concerned he rejected Malthusianism (on which Darwinism is based), and wrote of Malthus in terms of bitter personal hostility. The animus we may ignore, but the arguments are worth recapitulating. Pressure of population, he says, is the outcome of capitalism. On p. 645 of *Capital* Marx writes: " The labouring population . . . produces, along with the accumulation of capital produced by it, the means by which it is itself made relatively superfluous, is turned into a relatively surplus population, and it does this always to an increasing extent. This is a law of population peculiar to the capitalist mode of production, and in fact every special historic mode of production has its own special laws of population, historically valid within its limits alone. An abstract law of population exists for plants and animals only, and only in so far as man has not interfered

FOREWORD

with them." Later in the same chapter he says (in effect) that undue fertility is characteristic of poverty-stricken circumstances, and that with improved conditions the population difficulty tends to settle itself. We shall see that Loria says much the same thing, and shall consider the assertion presently. At a later date (1875) Marx writes somewhat more guardedly. In his *Criticism of the Gotha Programme* the reference to the Malthusian doctrine of population runs as follows: " But if I accept this law [the iron law of wages] as formulated by Lassalle, I must likewise accept its foundation. What is this foundation ? As F. A. Lange showed shortly after Lassalle's death, the iron law of wages is founded upon Malthus' theory of population, a theory which Lange himself espoused. Now if the iron law of wages be correct, it is impossible to abrogate it, even if we should do away with wage labour a hundred times over, for not the wage system alone, but every social system, must be governed by the law. Upon this foundation, for fifty years and more, economists have continued to demonstrate that socialism could never suppress poverty, which they regard as resulting from the nature of things. Socialism, they declare, can only generalise poverty, can only diffuse it simultaneously over the whole surface of society ! "

Does it not almost seem as if Marx, by 1875, had, for a moment at least, glimpsed the real difficulty ? For if we grant for the sake of argument that the excess of population under capitalism be only a relative excess, if we grant that each historic mode of production has its own special law of population, the question we have to ask ourselves as socialists is, " What will be the law of population under socialism ? " May not socialism tend to promote an *absolute* excess of population ? Will not natural increase, stimulated by easy circumstances, threaten the stability of the system unless the growth of population be deliberately checked ? Will not the inhabitants of each area have to specify some limit beyond which it is undesirable that the population of that area should increase ? Ways and means, social and individual, lie beyond our present scope. But in our opinion Paul Lafargue, Henry George, and many others who have written on this question, and who have endeavoured to meet the Malthusian difficulty by a simple denial of the facts upon which " Parson Malthus " grounded his theory, have displayed more zeal than knowledge. As Karl Pearson wrote thirty years ago : " Marx by abusing Malthus has not solved the population difficulty " ; and we agree with the same writer that " the acceptance of the law discovered by Malthus is an essential of any socialistic theory which pretends to be scientific"; but happily it is no longer true that "Kautsky seems to stand alone among socialists in accepting the Malthusian law and its consequences " (*The Ethic of Freethought*, 1888, pp. 438-9).

Loria's treatment of the subject is closely akin to that of Marx, though Loria differs from Marx in that he speaks with admiration, nay almost with veneration, of the author of *The Principles of Population*. As regards the main issue, Loria contends that while Malthus elucidated a profoundly important truth, he erred in respect of many of its applications. In present conditions, i.e. under capitalism, says Loria, there is no excess of population over food supply, but merely (in certain countries) an excess of people in relation to the privately owned capital which is able to secure profitable investment. Hence, as a result not of over-population but simply of capitalist conditions, we have in addition to

FOREWORD

the mass of the workers who obtain subsistence, on the one hand an owning class with a superfluity, and on the other a parasitic class of dependents, paupers, semi-criminals, and criminals. He contends, further, that Malthus' theory is invalidated by the ascertained fact that, as far as human beings are concerned, an excess of food over population does not necessarily lead to an increase in the birth rate—that a rising standard of life is nowadays apt to be characterised by diminished procreation. Speaking of certain postmalthusian applications of Malthus' theory, he writes (*Contemporary Social Problems*, p. 79): "Some also suggest various physiological expedients—the obscene abominations of the so-called neomalthusians—to limit population. Do they not see that there is no excess of mouths to be fed, and that procreation will of itself diminish with the amelioration of the condition of the working classes, without recourse to loathsome and unnatural practices?" In this passage, as repeatedly in his *Malthus*, Loria fails oddly (for so acute a mind) in his analysis of operating causes. As the result of a rising standard of life—consequent upon improved economic conditions among the proletariat—the workers, we are told (*Malthus*, p. 80), "become less prolific." Thus the growth of population is "automatically" regulated by economic means, and there is no need to have recourse to "physiological expedients" to limit population. Yet he nowhere endeavours to elucidate the working of this economic factor in the biologic field, or to show how it can possibly operate unless precisely in virtue of what he is so strangely and so inconsistently moved to condemn, viz. the deliberate application of increasing physiological knowledge by individual couples in order to regulate the number of their offspring. In a word, by birth control.

KARL MARX

As far as past stages of economic evolution are concerned, the transition from primitive tribal communism to slavery from slavery to serfdom and the guild system, and from these to capitalism, Loria himself insists that the prime motive force has been the pressure of increasing population on the means of subsistence. Thus in *Contemporary Social Problems* (pp. 128 et seq.) he writes: "We easily understand how evolution takes place in the sphere of economic phenomena provided we steadfastly hold in mind the simple premise that ceaseless increase in population makes necessary the occupation and cultivation of lands ever less fertile, hence requiring more efficacious means of production to combat the increasing resistance of matter. Given, therefore, a certain density of population and a certain degree of fertility of cultivated land, there is rendered not only possible, but also necessary, a determinate economic system permitting human labour to attain a commensurate productivity; but population increasing, and the necessity of cultivating less fertile lands becoming urgent, the economic system hitherto existing proves inadequate, since the degree of productivity which it permits to labour is insufficient to combat matter now become more rebellious. As the economic and productive system which corresponded with the preceding degree of the productivity of the soil has grown incompatible with the new and more exacting conditions, it must be supplanted by a better system. Then follows an epoch of social disintegration which destroys the superannuated form, from whose ashes a new structure arises; on the ruins of the shattered economic system is erected a new one which allows human nature to become more productive, and is therefore adapted, for a time, to combat the increasing resistance of matter. However, with each

FOREWORD

additional increment to population, a moment comes when it is necessary to bring under cultivation lands which are still more resistant, and for the development of which the prevailing economic system is found to be inadequate; consequently this system suffers the fate of those which have preceded it, and it is in turn destroyed to give place to a new and superior form."

The detailed application of these ideas is one of the main themes of Loria's *Analysis of Capitalist Property*. We learn, he says, from history and statistics that capitalistic property (the term is here used by Loria in the widest sense to include all the forms of property which render possible the exploitation of one human being by another) is everywhere and at all times due to one and the same cause, the suppression of free land. As long as there is any free land, as long as any man who so desires can take possession of a piece of land and develop it by his labour, capitalistic property is impossible, because no man will willingly work for another when he can establish himself for his own account on a piece of land without paying for it. Where there is free land, labour owns the means of production, so that agriculture is carried on by free peasants on small holdings, whilst manufacturing industry (in so far as this exists at such a stage) is in the hands of independent artisans. In these conditions labour is isolated, and isolated labour rarely produces anything more than the labourer's subsistence. The regular supplementary production of "income" is the characteristic feature of associated labour.

This brings us to *The Economic Synthesis*, a work which bears as sub-title " A Study of the Laws of Income." It is, Loria tells us, " the complement and the theoretic crown" of all his earlier writings. The meaning he attaches to the word income is, in truth, simple enough; but that meaning is the very core of Lorianism, just as surplus value is (for many) the very core of Marxism. Isolated labour, labour of the kind described in the last paragraph, produces, says Loria, first of all subsistence—the bare necessaries of life. In exceptionally favourable conditions even isolated labour may produce something more than this, and that something more is income. But as a rule, and more and more as population increases and land of diminishing fertility has to be brought under cultivation, *isolated* labour fails to produce anything beyond subsistence, fails to produce even that, so that it becomes necessary to have recourse to the superior productivity of *associated* labour. Now for this, since the natural man is averse from associated labour, some form of *coercion*, direct or indirect, is essential; and the history of all the developed economic systems that have hitherto prevailed, is the history, in one form or another, of the *coercion to associated labour*.

Income, in the Lorian sense of the term, is "the specific product of associated labour"; i.e., it is the surplus produced by labour because it is associated, over and above what the labourers could have produced in isolation. Working in isolation they produce, or theoretically might have produced, subsistence for themselves; associated they produce something more, which is income, and this accrues to those who control and direct the associating force. In primitive tribal communism that force emanates from the collectivity of economic equals, and the "undifferentiated income" is communally owned and consumed. But subsequently "differentiated income," received by non-labourers, makes its appearance. In slave-owning communities, differentiated

FOREWORD

income goes to the slave owners; in feudal serfdom, it accrues to the baronage; under modern capitalist conditions the dispossessed proletarian masses produce of course their own subsistence, and produce in addition income for the legal owners of land and capital. Slave owners, barons, capitalists, are in successive stages the "recipients of [differentiated] income." Throughout the history of these economic phases there has been a conflict between the interests of the labourers and those of the recipients of income, taking the form, in times of exceptional stress, of slave insurrections and slave wars, of jacqueries and ruthless reprisals by the baronage, of strikes and lock-outs. Here we have one aspect of what Loria terms "the struggle between subsistence and income," and this aspect coincides obviously enough with one aspect of the Marxist class struggle.

The association of labour is the prime cause of labour's enhanced productivity. But while the association increases productivity, the coercion that is requisite to secure association exercises a restrictive influence upon productivity, the restriction being more marked in proportion to the severity of the coercion. Thus the crude and harsh coercion of the slave-owning system makes slave labour (in part for psychological reasons dependent upon the mentality of the labourer) less productive than serf labour under the feudal system, wherein coercion was somewhat milder. In modern capitalism coercion, though still very real, is veiled, and for this reason (quite apart from the peculiar advantages of machinofacture) associated labour is more productive under capitalism. It is the superior productivity of each successive system which has rendered it victorious over its predecessor. With the dry light of economic science Loria displays for us the working of the type of production dominant to-day, the most effective system of production the world has yet known. Such is Loria's outline picture of the succession of economic phases.

It is impossible here to trace the Italian economist's detailed analysis of the causes which lead to the break up of one economic system and its replacement by another. Suffice it to say that in his view an important part is played by the action of those whom he calls "unproductive labourers," members of the educated caste living also on differentiated income, on portions of income reallotted by the primary recipients of income, whose interests, in the prosperous phase of any system of income, the educated caste is thus paid to serve. A typical service is that of the priestly order, which is maintained "to pervert the egoism" of the labourers, to delude them into the belief that they are pursuing their own better interests by peacefully and diligently producing income for the master class. But in the declining phase of any economic system (and Loria considers that the wage system of capitalism has now, despite its imposing appearance, actually entered its declining phase), the diminution of income curtails the amount available for reallotment to the unproductive labourers. Hence from supporters of the existing system they are speedily transformed into its active opponents. These "intellectuals" now make common cause with the labourers, the disinherited of the earth; and the old property system totters to its fall. He writes (*The Economic Foundations of Society*, p. 347): "All revolutions undertaken by the non-proprietary classes alone, without the support of the unproductive labourers, are . . . foredoomed to failure. The rebels, divided and disorganised, not at all sure of themselves and uncertain of the ends they would attain, soon fall

FOREWORD

back under the dominion of the proprietary class. . . . The ancient economy was not destroyed by the revolt of the slaves, nor was the ruin of the medieval economy effected by the armed uprising of the serfs. These two economic systems did not succumb until the clients of the Roman economy and the ecclesiastics of the medieval economy were induced by a falling-off of their share in the constantly decreasing revenues [income] to break their long-standing alliance with the revent holder [recipients of income] and to lend their support to the final revolt of the labouring classes."

To the Lorian theory of revolution we shall return in conclusion, after we have discussed the relationships of Loria to Marx. The theory involves tactical questions of the utmost interest and importance. Apart from these, the crux of the problem of transition to the co-operative commonwealth centres, as most thoughtful socialists are coming to see, around the question of the coercion to associated labour. A fundamental part of the socialist outlook is the belief that the existence of a special class of recipients of income, whether these be slave owners, feudal barons, or legal monopolists of land and capital, is not needful to modern civilisation. We affirm that the disappearance of such a class (though that class may have played a necessary part in social evolution) can now be witnessed by the enlightened without a single regret. But what is to ensure the continuance of that high social productivity which will be necessary to the maintenance of general wellbeing ? Now that our race is at length becoming truly self-conscious, will it be possible " to transform the economic natural force from the ruler of mankind to its servant " ? The closing sentences of *The Economic Synthesis* show in outline how Loria envisages that possibility: " The essential social contradiction can be eliminated, economic equilibrium can be established, only by means of a profound transformation, affecting not merely the process of distribution but also the process of production, relieving this latter process from the coercion which has hitherto environed it and restricted its efficiency; in other words, by the destruction of the coercive association of labour and its replacement by the free association of labour. Herein is to be found the supreme objective towards which must converge all the forces of social renovation." And in a terminal footnote he adds: " This is now understood by all the most enlightened economists, not excepting the socialists, who point out that a reform which effects no more than the distribution of income among the proletarians, while leaving unaffected the method by which that income is actually produced, would have no more than an extremely restricted and fugitive effect; and that a decisive and durable social renovation must be initiated by a radical metamorphosis in the process of production."

We have now to ask, what does Loria consider the most important elements of Marxist teaching? In his account of the *Communist Manifesto* (infra p. 43) he tells us that " this writing contains the whole Marxist system in miniature, and . . . supplies a critique of all doctrinaire, idealist, and utopian forms of socialism. Thus the *Manifesto* voices the two fundamentals of Marxism: the dependence of economic evolution upon the evolution of the instrument of production, in other words the *technicist determination of economics*; and the derivation of the political, moral, and ideal order from the economic order, in other words the *economic determination of sociology*—or, as we should express it to-day, historial

FOREWORD

materialism." On pp. 82 and 83 he tells us that we must "recognise in Marx the supreme merit of having been the first to introduce the evolutionary concept into the domain of sociology, the first to introduce it in the only form appropriate to social phenomena and social institutions; not as " an " unceasing and gradual upward movement," but as a " succession of age-long cycles rhythmically interrupted by revolutionary explosions." Speaking of Marx's "masterly investigation into the successive forms of the technical instrument, of productive machinery," he says that Marx may be termed " the Darwin of technology. . . . This physiology of industry, which is now the least studied and least appreciated of Marx's scientific labours, nevertheless constitutes his most considerable and most enduring contribution to science." Loria wrote his *Karl Marx* nearly two years before the publication of William Paul's *The State*, of which pp. 2 to 7, the section on " Man and Tools," is devoted to a restatement of this aspect of Marxism ; and the Italian economist is not acquainted with the thought-trend of Walton Newbold. As far as the young but rapidly growing and vigorous school of British Marxists is concerned, it is certainly no longer true that Marx's work as " the Darwin of technology " is the least studied and least appreciated of Marx's scientific labours.

To the class struggle Loria does not refer at any length in this essay on Karl Marx. We have already seen that he recognises the enormous part the class struggle has played in history; but he has throughout life remained the man of science, the man of the study ; he has never entered the arena as what the French term a " militant." In 1904, when the Italian Socialist Party wished him to be socialist parliamentary candidate for Turin, Loria refused on the ground that parliamentary life would interfere with his theoretical studies; and it may be that for these and other reasons he is less keenly impressed than are most left-wing socialists of the profound importance of diffusing among the workers awareness of the class struggle.

Economic determinism has been sufficiently considered in what has gone before. If in the present study Loria says less about it than about some of the other elements of Marxism, this is not because he considers it of minor importance, nor because he accepts it uncritically, but because he has devoted an entire volume to the exposition of this aspect of reality.

It remains, then, to discuss Loria's outlook on the Marxist theory of value. It is here that Lorianism will be most strenuously challenged by those more enthusiastic disciples of Marx who, even if they do not accept the dogma of Marx's infallibility, none the less regard the doctrine of value, based on the labour theory of value, as the very heart of Marxist socialism. We must remember that it is natural for persons who do not gain their subsistence by applying their labour power to the production of commodities, and whose claim to the title of 'workers" will nevertheless hardly be disputed, to question the labour theory of value. Bernard Shaw, for example, in his pamphlet *The Impossibilities of Anarchism*, protests that it is " natural for the [manual] labourer to insist that labour *ought to be* the measure of price, and that the just wage of labour is its average product; but the first lesson he has to learn in economics is that labour is not and never can be the measure of price under a competitive system. Not until the progress of socialism replaces competitive production and distribution with individual greed for its incentive, by collectivist production and distribution with fair play

FOREWORD

all round for its incentive, will the prices either of labour or of commodities represent their just value."

Leaving Shaw to the tender mercies of the orthodox Marxists who will not be slow to declare that if he means " value " he should not say " price," and that if he thinks that " price " and " value " are interchangeable terms he is not worth powder and shot, and without ourselves venturing to rush into the fray, we may suggest that our propagandists would be less inclined to make the Marxist theory of value an article of faith, " which faith except everyone do keep whole and undefiled without doubt he shall perish everlastingly "—if they could realise that the theory is perhaps no more than a difficult point of abstract economic doctrine which is not essential to the use of the conception of surplus value as a means of making the worker aware of the basic character of capitalist exploitation. Bernstein explains the matter very well in the book previously quoted (p. 35) : " Practical experience shows that in the production and distribution of commodities a part only of the community takes an active share, whilst another part consists of persons who either enjoy an income for services which have no direct relation to the process of production, or have an income without working at all. An essentially greater number of men thus live on the labour of all those engaged in production than are actively engaged in it, and income statistics show that the classes not actively engaged in production appropriate, moreover, a much greater share of the total produced than the ratio of their number to that of the actively producing class. The surplus labour of the latter is an empiric fact, demonstrable by experience, which needs no deductive proof. Whether the Marxist theory of value be correct or not, is quite immaterial to the proof of surplus labour. It is in this respect no demonstration, but only a means of analysis and illustration."

The professional economist, however, cannot rest content with these loose formulations. Loria feels that there is a void in the Marxist system, and it seems to us (though Loria nowhere tells us so in set terms) that the Lorian doctrine of differentiated income, the most essential part of the Italian economist's teaching, is really an attempt to restate the theory of surplus value in a form absolutely proof against enemy attack. Be this as it may, the conception, however interesting, is far less easy to convey to the uninstructed mind, and it is unlikely, for propaganda purposes, to replace the simple formula of surplus value. But is it not essential that those who undertake to teach socialist economics should themselves fully understand the objections to the Marxist theory of value, and that they should have a clear grasp of Loria's alternative doctrine of the nature of capitalist exploitation?

Let us return, in conclusion, to the Lorian theory of revolution. If we may summarise that theory in colloquial phraseology it is that, while economic evolution must pave the way for revolution, the final stages of revolution have been effected in the past, and can only be effected in the future, through the co-operation of "disgruntled intellectuals." These are the "unproductive labourers" of Loria's scheme, who have served as hirelings of the master class during the prosperous phase of an economic system; but in the declining phase of that system, when the diminution of income curtails the amount available for these secondary recipients of income, they turn against the primary recipients, their employers, make common cause with the subject class,

FOREWORD

and give the death-blow to the old order. This may possibly have been true of the fall of the slave economy, and it may possibly have been true of the fall of the medieval economy; but we do not think it is true that a revolution of the non-proprietary classes under capitalism is "foredoomed to failure" unless these classes secure the support of the unproductive labourers. Their support for a genuinely *proletarian* revolution can hardly be expected, on Loria's own theory. The intellectuals who aided in the overthrow of the slave economy, and the intellectuals who helped to subvert the feudal order and to promote the bourgeois and industrial revolution, did so, says Loria, in order to maintain their position as "recipients of income," to maintain their position as members of a privileged class. What have such as they to gain from a proletarian revolution, which will abolish class, will put an end to exploitation, will do away for ever with the private appropriation of income and surplus value? We need only turn our eyes eastward to see how such "intellectuals" will hail the revolution of the propertiless. Despite the onslaughts of the capitalist powers, the Russian Socialist Federative Soviet Republic has lived long enough to show the sort of help socialists may expect from the Kerenskys. Men of this calibre, "people whose interests lie in the opposite direction," even if they "are carried away by the new ideas and enter the lists for the new order of things" (Boudin, *The Theoretical System of Karl Marx*, 1918), are aghast when the real revolution comes, and endeavour to lay the red spectre they have helped to conjure up.

In truth, a revolution foredoomed to failure would be that of proletarians who should depend in large measure upon the support of disgruntled intellectuals. A serf's life was on the average better than that of a chattel slave; a wage labourer's life is on the average better than was that of slave or serf. But neither the replacement of slavery by feudalism, nor the replacement of feudalism by capitalism, secured the emancipation of labour in any adequate sense of that term. All that a proletarian revolution carried through with the help of middle-class intellectuals is likely to bring about is some form of Fabian collectivism or state capitalism —in a word, the servile state. As far as the *productive* labourers are concerned the revolution would be a sham. The form of the state might be revolutionised, but the authoritative state would endure, and production would be effected, not by the free, but by the coercive association of labour. What Loria has failed to recognise is that the conditions of the problem are now radically changed. As he says, in the old revolutions the rebels were divided and disorganised, were not sure of themselves, and were uncertain of the ends they would attain. As far as the workers were concerned, revolt only was possible, not revolution. It is otherwise to-day; and still more will it be otherwise the day after to-morrow. Thanks to the new forms of organisation now being worked out: thanks to industrial unionism and the growth of the workers committees and shop stewards movements; and thanks above all to independent working class education, which is forging the new weapons and simultaneously teaching the workers how to use them, which is fashioning the limbs of the co-operative commonwealth within the womb of the capitalist order—thanks to all these things, the workers of the day after to-morrow need not put their trust in the frail reed of the support of intellectuals. Once more we raise the Marxist slogan and cry : " The emancipation of the workers must be the work of

FOREWORD

the workers themselves." And if we modify another Marxist watchword, quoted on p. 87 below, that force is the midwife of every old society pregnant with a new one, it is only to say that, while we do not repudiate force (which the skilled accoucheur ever has in reserve), new times bring new methods. The self-educated workers of the future may have no occasion to use force, and certainly need not await the aid of Loria's unproductive labourers. For the day draws nigh, and on that day the workers will achieve their own salvation. They will achieve the salvation of all the workers, and indeed of all the world of man; but it will not be all the workers that will actively participate. No more will be possible than that there should be a considerable minority of educated workers. A minority they must inevitably remain until after the social revolution; but a little leaven can leaven a large lump. The midwife of revolution is not force but—independent working class education.

In a word, the "dynamogenic function" of which Loria speaks (infra pp. 89 and 90), attaches not to poverty but to slavery. The poor have seldom failed to realise their poverty, and poverty when extreme has at times led to revolt; but it is the new realisation of the *slavery* of wagedom that is organising the workers for the social revolution. By means of Marxist education "the proletarian is breaking his chains and entering upon an era of conscious and glorious freedom."

Do we seem to imply that there is no place in our movement for middle-class intellectuals? Such is not our meaning. They have played in the past a rôle of supreme importance, and may still have a notable part to play in the future. But the intellectuals for whom there is a place are not the kind of intellectuals described in

KARL MARX

Loria's theory of revolution, and the rôle of the intellectual is no longer the one which he assigns. It is not those intellectuals who are dissatisfied with their reallotment of income, not those who are discontented with their ration of loaves and fishes, not those who sigh for the vanishing cakes and ale, who will help the coming of the definitive social revolution. Rarely indeed, too, is the function of the socialist intellectual the function of leadership. To an increasing extent, under the new conditions, he tends to be no more than the fifth wheel of the revolutionary coach. The right sort of intellectual had a function in the past; it was to help the workers to overcome their division and disorganisation, to help them to be sure of themselves, to help them to clear views of the ends they must attain. That work is afoot. The ferment has been created: created by such men as Marx, whose abilities would have secured him ease, comfort, wealth, had he made his peace with bourgeoisdom, but who was a revolutionist by deliberate choice; by such men as Engels, a well-to-do manufacturer; by such men as Loria himself, a university professor; by such men as the American, Scott Nearing, who recently forfeited his academic position because he would not keep the class struggle out of his lectures on economics. Can it be said that men like Herzen, Bakunin, and Kropotkin, have been, or that men like Trotzky and Lenin are, the disgruntled intellectuals of Loria's theory of revolution? Quite apart from leadership under such peculiar conditions as obtain in Russia, there is work for socialist intellectuals, the work of promoting independent working-class education, the work of assisting in the spread of the ferment generated by the writings of earlier revolutionary thinkers. Our conviction that we ourselves, declassed bourgeois, have a modest function, that though

FOREWORD

not part of the team, not even spokes of a fifth wheel, we may at least help to complete the outfit as little dogs under the waggon, is witnessed by our translation of Achille Loria's monograph on Karl Marx.

EDEN AND CEDAR PAUL.

LONDON,
The Centenary of Karl Marx.

KARL MARX
A SKETCH

BY
ACHILLE LORIA

KARL MARX

IT is unquestionably one of the strangest of anomalies exhibited by the polychrome flora of human thought that revolutionary blossoms should so frequently spring from aristocratic seeds, and that the most incendiary and rebellious spirits should emerge from a domestic and social environment compounded of conservatism and reaction. Yet when we look closely into the matter, we find it less strange than it may have appeared at first sight. It is, in fact, not difficult to understand that those only who live in a certain milieu can fully apprehend its vices and its constitutional defects, which are hidden as by a cloud from those who live elsewhere. It is true enough that many dwellers in the perverted environment lack the intelligence which would enable them to understand its defects. Others, again, are induced by considerations of personal advantage to close their eyes to the evils they discern, or cynically to ignore them. But if a man who grows to maturity in such an environment be at once intelligent and free from base elements, the sight of the evil medium from which he himself has sprung will arouse in his mind a righteous wrath and a spirit of indomitable rebellion, will transform the easy-going and cheerful patrician into the prophet and the revolutionary. Such has been the lot of the great rebels of the world, of men like Dante, Voltaire, Byron, Kropotkin, and Tolstoi, who all sprang

KARL MARX

from the gentle class, and whose birthright placed them among the owners of property. Similar was the lot of Karl Marx.

It would, indeed, be difficult to imagine a more typically refined and aristocratic entourage than the one wherein the future high priest of the revolution was born and passed his early years. He was born at Treves on May 5, 1818. His ancestors on both sides had been distinguished rabbis, famed for their commentaries on the scriptures. The father's family was originally known as Mordechai, whilst the mother's family, Pressburg by name, had come from Hungary to settle in Holland. His father, an employee in the state service, became a Christian, and the whole family was baptised when Karl was five years of age. As he grew up, the young man was an intimate in the best houses of the district, and one of his closest friends was Edgar von Westphalen, who subsequently became a member of the reactionary Manteuffel ministry. In 1843 Marx married Westphalen's sister, the beautiful and brilliant Jenny. The match proved well assorted, and was blessed by a love so intense and so unfailing as to lead a certain German pastor to say that it had been ratified in heaven. Thus by origin Marx belonged to an extremely ancient stock devoted to the accumulation of wealth, whilst his marriage united him to the race of German feudatories, fierce paladins of the throne and of the altar. Is it not then truly remarkable that from such an environment, eminently calculated to foster ideas of obscurantism and reaction, there should emerge the most brilliant, most consistent, and most invincible example of a thinker and revolutionary agitator?

Unquestionably, Marx's thought, essentially slow-moving, laborious, and ever subjected to a rigorous process of self-criticism, does not seem at first sight characteristically negational and rebellious. In youth, indeed, he was still no more than the earnest student. Engels tells us that he closed his university career at Bonn in 1841 by writing a brilliant thesis upon the philosophy of Epicurus, while in leisure moments Marx penned verses of no mean order. These latter compositions display numerous defects of style; they are heavy and turgid; the movement is sluggish; their sonorous gravity reminds the reader of a company of medieval warriors in heavy armour mounting the grand staircase: but they are none the less distinguished by remarkable profundity of thought, and they may be looked upon as versified philosophy rather than as poetry in the proper sense of the term. In the following year we find Marx at Cologne as editor of the "Rhenish Gazette." His editorials, it is true, were at first devoted to harmless topics of general interest; but he soon began to turn his attention to social questions, such as forest thefts, the subdivision of landed property, the condition of the peasantry in the Moselle district, and French socialism. To this last doctrine, the editor declared himself adverse, while professing a great personal admiration for Proudhon. But the discussion upon socialism revealed to him his own ignorance and incompetence, and induced him to withdraw from the journalistic arena that he might devote himself to study. An excuse for resigning his editorship was furnished in 1843, when the "Rhenish Gazette" found it necessary to assume an extremely cautious tone in order to avoid the attentions of the police.

But, like all the more brilliant and free-spirited among his contemporaries, he soon found himself incommoded by the obscurantism of Prussia, and, accompanied by

KARL MARX

his young wife, he hastened to Paris, the city of light, where there shortly assembled a circle of intellectual rebels from all lands—France, Germany, England, Italy, and Russia. The Russians predominated, and indeed we learn from Marx himself that the most fervent of his disciples at this date were drawn from among the scions of the Russian nobility and upper bourgeoisie, who when they returned to their country were unhesitatingly to become the sycophants of authority. In this cohort of spiritual rebels he assumed from the first the position of dictator, and none competed for the crown with the revolutionary Cæsar. People were already beginning to talk of the Marxists, and the police made a black cross against the name of a Parisian café where the associates of Marx were wont to assemble. He struck up a friendship with Heinrich Heine, and one day, accompanied by his staff, he paid a formal visit to the poet and declared that the latter ought to divide among the exiles the pension granted him by Guizot, to which suggestion Heine cynically replied that he could spend the pension more profitably upon himself. Marx had a yet closer intimacy with Proudhon, with whom he passed long evenings talking about Hegel and discussing the problems of socialism; but this friendship was destined ere long to be replaced by fierce hostility, aroused by fundamental differences of opinion. In 1844, in conjunction with Arnold Ruge, Marx founded the " Franco-German Year Book," of which, however, there appeared but one volume, containing writings by Marx himself on the philosophy of law and upon the Jews, in addition to letters from Holland, and articles by Engels, Heine, Freiligrath, and other more or less rebellious spirits.

These outward activities represent nothing more than

an interlude or partial episode in the series of his essential occupations, science and philosophy. Engels' contribution to the "Year Book," a criticism of political economy, initiated between the two thinkers a friendship which time was to strengthen and to render indissoluble. The first fruit of this friendship was a joint work entitled *The Holy Family*, a criticism of the philosophy of Bruno Bauer and his followers (1845), stuffed with sallies and orphic sayings of doubtful taste and still more doubtful value. The young men next turned to a weightier task, a criticism of posthegelian philosophy, which filled two huge octavo manuscript volumes, but has never found a publisher. Nevertheless, Marx tells us, this enormous labour cannot be regarded as utterly wasted, for it enabled the writers to gain an understanding of themselves, and traced the lines by which henceforward they were to be safely guided through the labyrinth of social investigation.

But revolutionary agitation (which Marx continued even amid his philosophical meditations), and the editorship of the definitely antiprussian journal "Forward," now attracted the hostile attention of the Prussian government, upon whose demand, in January, 1845, Guizot suppressed the periodical and expelled Marx from France. Marx removed to Brussels, where Engels was living, and for the first time devoted himself to prolonged and profound labours. In the year 1847, he published in the Belgian capital his book *The Poverty of Philosophy, a Reply to Proudhon's Philosophy of Poverty*, a harsh criticism of the "economic contradictions" of his rival. Marx reproached Proudhon for complete ignorance of that Hegelian philosophy which Proudhon tried to apply to economics, and reproached the French socialist yet more for arbitrary and fallacious expositions, for the idealisation of a tortuous series of fantastic categories (division of labour, machines, competition, rent, etc.), declaring that Proudhon confined himself in each case to an examination of the good and the bad effects without ever troubling to throw light upon the nature of the phenomena under consideration or upon the course of their formation and development. The criticism is apt, but might well rebound upon Marx himself, enmeshed at this epoch in a series of categories whose progressive evolution he arbitrarily asserted. Further, Marx fiercely criticised Proudhon's theory of " constituted value," according to which the reduction of value to labour cannot be effected in extant society, and must be deferred to the future society, fashioned in the brain of the thinker. It is well to point out that Marx, though in the first volume of *Capital* he conceives the reduction of value to the quantity of effective labour to be one of the immanent laws of capitalist economy, nevertheless admits in the third volume that in the capitalist economic phase value neither is nor can be reduced to the quantity of labour, and that value as measured by labour is merely an archetype or suprasensible entity, but not a concrete reality. Substantially this means that Marx's labour measure of value is, after all, not essentially different from the constituted value of Proudhon. But amid these unjust or excessive criticisms, Marx's book gives utterance to the idea, profoundly true, and at that time practically original, that economic relationships are no mere arbitrary products or derivatives of human will, but are the inevitable issue of the existing condition of the forces of production. The deduction drawn from this is that utopian socialism, which exhausts itself in futile declamations or in yet more futile imaginary reconstructions of the social order, must yield place to scientific socialism, wholly devoted to the analysis of the necessary process of economic evolution and to the possibility of accelerating that evolution.

The same idea can be read between the lines of the *Lecture on Free Exchange* delivered by Marx at Brussels on January 9, 1849. Herein he asserted that socialism ought to declare in favour of freedom of trade, for this, hastening the dissolution of the old nationalities and accentuating the contrast between the bourgeoisie and the proletariat, would precipitate the dissolution of the capitalist economy. But the idea is affirmed far more categorically in the *Manifesto of the Communist Party*, the joint composition of Engels and Marx, published in the year 1848, embodying the first and most decisive formulation of the latter's teaching. Even though some of his special theories, subsequently to secure fuller development in *Capital*, are but cursorily sketched in the *Manifesto*, even though some of these theories (for example, the theory of wages, stated to be the price of " wage labour " instead of being the price of " labour power ") are still in an undeveloped and imperfect state, it is nevertheless true that this writing contains the whole Marxist system in miniature, and that it supplies a critique of all doctrinaire, idealist, and utopian forms of socialism. Thus the *Manifesto* voices the two fundamentals of Marxism: the dependence of economic evolution upon the evolution of the instrument of production, in other words the *technicist determination of economics*, and the derivation of the political, moral, and ideal order from the economic order, in other words the *economic determination of sociology*—or, as we should express it to-day, historical materialism. This dependence of the political order upon the economic order reading as it does to the concentration of political power in the hands of those who hold economic power, or in the hands of their representatives and agents, renders absurd the idea of effecting by peaceful political means any amelioration in the condition of the proletarian classes and indicates to the dispossessed that revolution is their only hope of salvation. To revolution, then, or to the compact federation which can alone pave the way for revolution, the *Manifesto* incites the sufferers of the world with the historic phrase : " Workers of the world, unite." The epoch-making significance of the *Manifesto* is not to-day disputed by the most resolute adversaries of that document. It is, in fact, the Declaration of Rights of the Fourth Estate, the Magna Charta of the revolutionary proletariat, the oriflamme of fire and blood, the standard round which the insurrectionary phalanxes have ever since mustered.

Hardly had the message been launched upon the world when the young leader hoped to translate it into action, for the movements of 1848 and 1849 led the rebel masses to entertain new and bolder aspirations. Expelled from Belgium, Marx first went to Paris, and hastened thence to his German homeland, now in a ferment, assuming there editorial charge of the " New Rhenish Gazette." But although the skill of the able editor was for a brief period successful in saving the barque of the imperilled gazette from the waves of police persecution, a day soon arrived when the situation became untenable. An appeal to the German people published in the columns of the journal advocating a refusal to pay taxes led to its suppression and to two criminal charges against the editor. Triumphantly acquitted by the Cologne jury, but none the less exiled by the Prussian government, he immediately returned to Paris, where it seemed to his restless imagination that events were taking a more favourable turn. But France proved a no securer refuge than Germany, and the Parisian government propounded to our agitator a peremptory dilemma, internment in the remote department of Morbihan or exile from France. He was not likely to hesitate in his choice, and indeed at this juncture was glad to accept an invitation from the executive committee of the Communist Party, then centred in London, to remove with his devoted wife to that great metropolis (1849).

Here the saddest trials awaited him, for poverty, gloomy companion, sat ever at his board from the day of his entry into the British capital down to the hour of his last breath. One after another of his children died in the unwholesome dwellings of his exile, and he was forced to beg from friends and comrades the scanty coins needed to pay for their burial; he and his family had to make the best of a diet of bread and potatoes; he was forced to pawn his watch and his clothing, to sell his books, to tramp the streets in search of any help that might offer; the day came when, under the lash of hunger, he was compelled to contemplate seeking work as railway clerk, of placing his daughters out to service, of making them governesses or actresses, whilst himself retiring with his unhappy wife to dwell in the proletarian quarter of Whitechapel.

The severity of these sufferings did much to add a tinge of gall to a character naturally acerb, a character which amid the upheavals and horrors of exile frequently showed itself far from amiable. Mingled sentiments of grief and anger fill our minds when, in Marx's private letters to Engels, we trace the manifestations of this harshness, which left him unmoved by the misfortunes of his dearest friends, which led him to make any use he could of these friends and then to overwhelm them with reproaches and accusations, which showed itself (and this is the worst of all) in a jealous hatred of comrades less unfortunate than himself. Deplorable from every point of view was his conduct towards Freiligrath and Lassalle, in especial towards Lassalle, who had shown him the utmost friendliness, had given him ample financial assistance, had entertained him in Berlin, had helped him to find a publisher; for Marx subsequently censured Lassalle's works with much acrimony, beheld his triumphs askance, and commented upon the incidents of Lassalle's death in a tone of tepid apology. But you well-fed folk who amid easy circumstances are studying the life of our agitator, be not too ready to blame him, and before stoning him bethink yourselves of all the miseries the exile must suffer, of all the tortures amid which he must bear his cross.

Vainly did he endeavour by hard work to free himself from the sad restraints of poverty. It is true he was able to place articles with the "New York Tribune," writing for this paper essays on political, economic, and financial questions, which secured much appreciation. But the pay was only one pound per article, and he could write but one article a week. Collaboration in the production of an American encyclopædia, to be paid at the rate of two dollars a page, seemed to promise more ample funds, and with feverish anxiety he devoted himself to the production of articles on the most varied topics, well stored with facts. But this source of income, limited at best, was suddenly interrupted by the outbreak of the American civil war. The loss was not adequately compensated by the possibility of occasionally inserting some poorly paid contribution in a German newspaper like the " New Oder Gazette " or in one of the Viennese periodicals.

He was lucky in that certain turns of fortune favoured him from those sources of property and inheritance which he condemned and attacked with such persistence and vehemence. He had a legacy from his mother-in-law; a legacy from his mother; a trifling legacy from an aunt; and Wilhelm Wolff, a companion in exile, bequeathed him £800. An uncle in Holland, whom he had begged for some trifling help, gave him £160; from Lassalle and Freiligrath came generous gifts; and Droncke, another companion in exile, gave £250 to enable him to complete the scientific work on which he was engaged. But none of these casual resources, however extensive, would have saved him from ruin had it not been for the providential assistance of his friend Friedrich Engels, who applied himself to the care of Marx with inexhaustible generosity, and with the tenderness of a woman. Engels, indeed, will secure a splendid place in the history of socialist thought, were it only because of the way in which he devoted himself to Marx. It was through Engels that Marx was enabled to continue his studies and to complete the work which is his title to eternal fame. Engels, a well-to-do cotton spinner at Manchester, gladly responded to his friend's unremitting requests for aid, succouring him in every emergency. Engels was an expert upon military topics, and penned articles which Marx passed on to the " Tribune " and to the encyclopædia, articles for which Marx was paid; Engels sent Marx weekly subsidies, and frequently despatched gifts of port wine; he made presents of £100 or £150 at a time; and at length, when his business prospered, he gave his friend a regular allowance of £350 a year.

KARL MARX

Not even these strokes of good luck sufficed, it is true, to restore a satisfactory balance to Marx's finances, for he was a bad manager, and the disorder was probably incurable. However, they enabled our thinker to furnish aid to companions yet more unfortunate, to Pieper, Eccarius, and Dupont; they enabled him to escape from the worst extremities of poverty and to establish himself in life under conditions more worthy of an honest and respectable bourgeois. He was able to move from the decayed neighbourhood of Soho Square and to settle in Maitland Park Road on Haverstock Hill; it became possible for him to secure a good education for his daughters, to have them taught French and Italian, drawing and music; he could weigh the financial status of aspirants to their hands, and could choose Lafargue and Longuet, who were comparatively well off. He often went to the theatre, and with one of his daughters he attended at the Society of Arts a soirée graced by the presence of royalty; from time to time he took his family to the seaside; he liked his wife to sign herself " Jenny, née Baronne de Westphalen "; he was well received in affluent circles, and was frequently consulted by the " Times " upon financial affairs; finally he accepted the office of constable of the vestry of St. Pancras, taking the customary oath, and donning the regulation uniform on gala occasions.

Nevertheless, neither this final settlement in a foreign land nor the persecution he suffered from the government of his own country could destroy or even lessen his devotion to Germany. To the day of his death he remained a faithful child of the fatherland, for which he hoped the greatest of futures. He sang the praises of German music and literature; he delighted in German victories and German expansion; he dreaded a weakening of German protectionism which might strengthen the commercial hegemony of Britain; and in 1870 he refused to sign an appeal in favour of peace unless it were definitely stated that Germany was waging a purely defensive war. The French and Russian exiles in London were indignant, and circulated whispers that Marx was a Prussian emissary, and had received a bribe of £10,000. An idle tale! It is true that among German conservatives and among the beneficiaries of Germany there could not be found a supporter more sincere and more fervent than was this proscribed rebel. But he was no paladin on behalf of Prussian imperialism, as we can learn beyond dispute from a letter he sent to the "Daily News" in 1878 denouncing Bismarckian ambitions and the Bismarckian expansionist policy as a growing peril.

Yet the supreme aim of his activity and his life. enormously transcended the circumscribed range of country and of nation, for he aspired to a loftier goal, to the organisation of the mental and manual workers of all countries so that they might constitute a united revolutionary force. Within a brief time of his arrival in the British metropolis he again became the chief, nay the dictator, of a circle to which none could be admitted without passing a severe examination as to knowledge of science in general and of political economy in particular, an examination so rigorous that even Wilhelm Liebknecht was unable at first to satisfy its requirements, an examination that was physical as well as mental, for the aspirants were subjected (rejoice, shade of Lombroso!) to precise craniometrical tests. Thus our thinker, crowned as if by divine right with a kind of imperial halo, exercised undisputed sway over the troop of exiles, Pieper, Bauer, Blind, Biskamp, Eccarius, Liebknecht, Freiligrath, Cesare Orsini (brother of the regicide), and even over the revolutionary agitators in Germany. Soon, however, his mind was invaded and dominated by a yet more ambitious design, for he planned the formation of a society which should unite the proletarians of all the world into one formidable International, to resist the aggressions of capital and to work for the destruction of the capitalist system. It was at first an association of modest proportions, consisting merely of a few revolutionaries assembled in London. Marx absolutely refused the chairmanship, contenting himself with the post, ostensibly less important, of delegate for the German section. From the first formation of the new federation Marx did his utmost to counteract the influence of Mazzini, for Mazzini, through the instrumentality of two of his followers, Fontana and the elder Wolff, wished to inspire the International with his idealist conceptions and to initiate it into the secrets of conspiracy. Marx, on the other hand, was unwearying in his efforts to advocate his own view that material interests preponderate, and that these interests must be publicly asserted and defended in the arena of history. Soon the federation established branches in France, Germany, the United States, and even the Latin countries; and this involved for Marx, who was really the chief, a mass of work in the way of organisation, and of struggle against those who held conflicting views. Everywhere, in fact, he had to encounter trends differing from his own, and differing no less extensively one from another owing to the varying characters of the countries concerned. In Germany he had to fight the opportunism of Lassalle, a man inclined to compromises and to elastic unions with constituted authority. In France anti-intellectual tendencies were already manifest, so that there was an inclination to restrict the socialist outlook to an aspiration for immediately practical labour legislation of minor importance. In Italy and in Spain Marx's troubles arose from the anarchist tendencies characteristic of those countries, tendencies fostered by the propaganda of Bakunin. As against these divergent aims, Marx, with inflexible tenacity, maintained his own programme with the utmost rigour, insisting that it was essential to federate the proletarian forces of the world into an invincible organisation which in all possible ways, by strikes, by parliamentary and legal methods, but also by force should need arise, should deliver onslaughts upon the bourgeoisie and upon constituted authority, should exact concessions of increasing importance, and should ultimately secure a complete triumph. The proletarians of the two hemispheres were not slow to accept the programme; and this man who was himself suffering from actual hunger, now secured a great position as a thinker, so that the operatives of Paris, New York, and Düsseldorf did honour to his name.

These activities, however, did not completely interrupt his intellectual labours, for during the period at which we have now arrived he published in the "New York Tribune" a series of articles upon *Revolution and Counter-revolution in Germany* and upon *Political Struggles in France*. In 1852, in "The Revolution," published in the German tongue in New York, there had appeared the article *The Eighteenth Brumaire of Louis Bonaparte.* Substantially these writings are an application of the materialist conception of history to the more conspicuous events of the recent political history of Germany and of France. In addition, Marx published in the "Tribune" a series of articles of a more distinctively

KARL MARX

political character, dealing with *The Eastern Question*, displaying marvellous erudition and a wonderful power of forecasting events.

Nevertheless, the organisation of the proletariat, and his journalistic labours, however intense and however weighty, did not represent in the life of Marx anything more than a vexatious parenthesis or a regrettable delay in the fulfilment of the supreme task he had set before himself from the very outset of his life in Britain. Hardly, in fact, had Marx settled down in the wonderful town of London, to the economist so inexhaustible a field for study and experience, than he proposed to rebuild from the foundations the entire edifice of his economic and statistical knowledge, which was at that time comparatively small when contrasted with the vast extent of his preliminary readings in philosophy. In the British Museum library, therefore, he plunged into the study of the classical economists of the island realm, showing inexhaustible patience in tracing the earliest and most trifling ramifications of economic science.

Beginning with the study of the theory of rent, he went on to the study of money, of the relationship between the quantity of metal in circulation and the rate of exchange, of the influence of bank reserves upon prices, and so forth. He then devoted himself to the theories of value, profit, interest, and population. Simultaneously he studied without remission statistics, blue books, ministerial and parliamentary concerns. From all this gigantic toil he derived the materials for the writing of the work which was henceforward to be at once the sorrow and the joy of his life. His first intention was to limit himself to a critical history of political economy, or a detailed analysis of the theories which he had so often enunciated, as well as of the lacunae which had become apparent in them. But an unexpected result issued from the mental contact with this huge mass of science and analysis, for he believed that he had made a splendid and startling discovery whereby the sacred theory of profit could be utterly exploded. Now, therefore, he outlined the design of his great work, which was to consist of two parts: a first, historico-critical, intended to elucidate the different forms of the theory of profit as expounded by the various British economists; and a second, theoretical and constructive, which was to announce to the world the author's own doctrine. This method of exposition is substantially identical with that followed by Böhm-Bawerk in his *Capital and Interest*, and it corresponds moreover to the immediate requirements of the investigation, which ought to begin with the study of prevailing opinions and doctrines, and then only proceed to innovation. But a more attentive examination of the question soon convinced Marx that this would not be the most efficacious method of furnishing a theoretical reproduction of actualities, since, to this end, we must let the phenomena tell their own tale before we proceed to call to account those who have already analysed them, and before we draw attention to the ways in which their conception of the facts diverges from that which reality, when directly questioned, reveals. The method has ever been preferred by the most gifted theorists, and has been applied by Bergson with admirable dexterity in his *Creative Evolution*. Marx, therefore, never weary of destroying and refashioning, inverted his original design, and promptly began the study and analysis of concrete phenomena, to proceed then only to a criticism of the theories of his precursors. It was in accordance with such criteria that he wrote his *Criticism of Political Economy*, of which the first instalment was published at Berlin in 1859.

The most notable portion of this work is the preface, which contains the first statement of the theory of historical materialism. The relationships of men in social life, says Marx, are determined by the conditions of production, are necessary relationships independent of the individual will; these determined relationships constitute the real foundation upon which is erected the legislative, political, moral, and religious superstructure of every age. The relationships of production, or the economic relationships prevailing at a given period, are a natural and necessary outcome of the method of production, or rather of the historic phase of the instrument of production. But sooner or later the further development of the productive forces generates a new configuration in technical method, a configuration incompatible with the prevailing relationships of production, those correlative to the productive order hitherto dominant. There then occurs an explosion, a social revolution, which disintegrates economic relationships, and, by ricochet, disintegrates existing social relationships, replacing them by better economic relationships, adequate to the new and more highly evolved phase of the productive instrument. In broad outline it may be said that economic evolution has exhibited four progressive phases; the Asiatic economy, the classical economy, the feudalist economy, and the modern bourgeois or capitalist economy. The evolution of the productive instrument, never arrested in its secular march, will in due course renew the eternally recurrent opposition between the method of production and the relationships of production, rendering these incompatible. Once more will come an explosion, the last of the great social convulsions, whereby the bourgeois economic order will be overthrown and will be replaced by the co-operative commonwealth. This new development will close the primary epoch of the history of human society.

But the work we are discussing is further noteworthy inasmuch as it reflects a special phase of our author's thought, a thought which never ceased to exhibit a struggle between opposing trends and was ever oppressed by their contrast. The book, in fact, shows Marx continually involved in antiquated Hegelian machinery, or proceeding through a chain of categories evolving one from another—capital, landed property, the wage system, the state, foreign commerce, the world market. From each of these categories we may infer how the process of their successive development is accomplished. We are led to infer that the wage system is the outcome of landed proprietorship, for the expropriation of the peasant proprietors produces the proletarianised masses offering labour power for sale ; and we are led to infer that the constitution of the world market is the crown and the epilogue of modern capitalist economy. In fact, according to Marx, the historic mission of capitalism based upon wage labour, whose origins go back to the sixteenth century, is the creation of the world market. The world market is now devoted to the colonisation of California and Australia and to the opening of trading ports in China and Japan ; its creation marks the climax of capitalism's historic mission, and indicates the approaching end of the economic form which was destined to fulfil it. Now these ideas, in themselves arbitrary and fantastic, show how Marx's thought at that epoch was still in an undecided or amphibious phase, in which the torrid sun of British economic science had not as yet succeeded in totally dispelling the fogs of German philosophy. But another incompatibility lessens the value of the book or diminishes its doctrinal efficacy; for Marx, at this stage of his studies, invariably gave to the history of doctrine too preponderant a place, introducing it insistently into the course of his own exposition, which was thus deprived of continuity and weakened in force.

Further, the book we are considering did not directly bear upon any of the social questions which strongly arouse public interest, but was restricted to the study of two theories whose importance at first sight seems purely academic, the theory of value and the theory of money. Marx contended that the value of commodities is exclusively determined by the quantity of labour incorporated into them; he traced the affiliations of this thesis with the work of its first enunciators in Italy and in England; but he did not offer any reasoned demonstration of its truth. On the contrary, he frankly recognised that this contention is full of contradictions alike theoretical and practical, contradictions that appear insoluble; but he promised to vanquish them in the subsequent course of his exposition. Far more noteworthy is the chapter on money, for it contains a masterly criticism of the quantitative theory of Ricardo, and an effective refutation of the " labour notes " idea of Bray, Gray, Proudhon, and others. According to this plan, every producer performing a certain quantum of labour would receive from the state a voucher entitling him to obtain from other producers the result of an equal quantum of labour; but the suggestion implies complete ignorance of the intrinsic conditions of the individualistic economy, wherein each producer creates an object without any certainty that there will be a market for it, or that it represents a real utility and will fetch a definite price. It obviously follows that the producer cannot be sure that he will be able to sell the article which he has produced, or that he will be able to transform it into anything with universal purchasing power; the product has to be baptised or sanctioned by the market, which alone has power to stamp it as useful by purchasing it. Now the "labour note" system claims that it can forcibly dispense with the market by supplying to the producer of an article whose utility and saleable value has not been recognised by the market, a universally available purchasing power. The practical outcome of this forcible method is that the producer of a useless article can by means of his "labour note" secure for himself a useful article, whereas the producer of this latter will not in turn be able to exchange his own "labour note" for any object possessing utility; that is to say, the article made by the first producer will find no purchaser, and the "labour note" of the second producer will effect no purchase. This is inevitable, for the proposed reform is inconsistent, eclectic, and incomplete, since it pretends to socialise exchange while maintaining production and distribution upon their old individualistic basis, and overlooks the incongruity of any such supposition. The "labour note" system cannot rationally be instituted until production has been socialised, or until the state shall impose upon each individual the production of a specified quantity and quality of commodities, correlatively imposing upon the consumer the obligation to acquire these. In such conditions, however, we could no longer speak of commodities or of exchange, for these phenomena belong exclusively to an individualistic economy and would have no place in a socialised economy.

This means that the reform of exchange by the suppression of profit can only be effected by the suppression of exchange itself, by the institution of the co-operative commonwealth. Indeed, Robert Owen, who proposed the " labour note " system in 1832, and was the most brilliant of its advocates, clearly recognised this difficulty, and understood that the socialisation of production would be an indispensable preliminary to the adoption of the plan. It was the impatience of his disciples which forced him to inaugurate the system within the framework of the capitalist economy by founding the National Equitable Labour Exchange. The logic of facts gave a patent demonstration of the irrationality of the attempt; and Owen, saddened and humiliated, was compelled to witness the failure of the new institution.

It will readily be understood that these abstruse and abstract investigations, devoid as they are of any tangible connection with the burning problems of property, were not likely to arouse interest among the members of the party. Nothing could be more natural than the tone of hopeless discouragement with which the volume was greeted even by the author's most devoted friends. Liebknecht, for example, declared that he had never before experienced so great a disappointment. Biskamp enquired what on earth it was all about; Burgers deplored that Marx should have published a work so dull and fragmentary. It is true that the book had a moderate sale; Rau quoted it in his treatise; certain Russian and American economists made it the subject of profound studies. Nevertheless, the publisher refused to proceed with the issue.

Hardly had this literary bickering come to an end when Marx became involved in a violent quarrel with the distinguished naturalist Karl Vogt, who publicly charged him with setting snares for the German exiles and with having sordid relationships with the police. Marx replied with a savage booklet entitled *Herr Vogt* (London, 1860). The style of this polemic writing is intolerably vulgar; but in other respects the book is noteworthy, for it contains interesting revelations anent the Italian campaign and the relationships between Turin and the Tuileries. We must remember, moreover, that the accusation here launched against Vogt, that he was in the pay of the Second Empire, was subsequently confirmed beyond dispute, for in 1871 among the ruins of the Tuileries there was found a receipt for frs. 40,000 which had been paid over to Vogt.

But scientific failures, personal contests, persistent and distressing domestic discomforts, seemed to inspire our athlete with renewed strength for the continuance of the work he had begun. Nevertheless, profiting by experience, he decided upon a yet further modification in the plan of his book, resolving to defer to its final section all historico-critical disquisitions, and to concentrate his energies upon the positive analysis of concrete reality. Further, being prevented by frequent illness from tackling the more difficult themes of pure economics, he devoted these long intervals of comparative leisure to statistical investigations and to the perusal of factory inspectors' reports, of white books and of blue books, and he plunged into the study of the economic history of Great Britain, so that it became possible for him to interleave the pages of abstract theory, necessarily difficult to understand, with pages that are really living, pages that vibrate with the reflex of reality. At length, abandoning the method he had previously followed of publishing fragmentary essays, he decided to rewrite the work throughout before sending it to press.

KARL MARX

After several years of incredible labour, the days being devoted to reading in the British Museum library, and the nights (for he often went on writing until four in the morning) to literary composition; falling again and again beneath the burden of his cross, but ever rising to his feet once more, thanks to the demon within urging him on and thanks also to the sustaining hand of his incomparable friend; he at length completed his task, and in the spring of 1867 sailed for Hamburg with the manuscript of the first volume of *Capital*, which he entrusted to Meissner for publication. In Hamburg he passed pleasant days with Dr. Kugelmann, a friend and fervent admirer, and with various officials, generals, and bankers; he was visited by a lawyer named Warnebold, an emissary from Bismarck, who, acting on the minister's instructions, exhorted him "to employ his brilliant talents for the advantage of the German people." Before long, however, he returned to London, where he earnestly devoted himself to giving the last touches to his book, which was finally issued from the press in the autumn of the same year.

Thus was at length given to the world the monumental work destined to revolutionise sociological thought, and to give a new and higher trend, not to socialism alone, but to political economy itself. To sum up its drift very briefly, we may say that the argument follows three chief lines, value, machinery, and primitive accumulation. He set out from the fundamental principle (a principle which the philosopher Krause had declared to be as important to political economy as the fall of heavy bodies is important to physics) that the value of products is measured by the mass of labour incorporated into them, and drew the conclusion that the profit of capital is nothing other than the materialisation of a quantity of labour expended by the worker, and is in other words unpaid labour, stolen and usurped income. The worker, that is to say, transmits into the product a value equal to the quantity of labour incorporated therein, but receives from the capitalist a value less than this, a value equal to the quantity of labour embodied in the commodities necessary to reproduce the energy expended by the worker. Now the difference between the value of the product (that is to say the quantity of labour transmitted by the worker into the product) and the value of the labour power (that is to say the quantity of labour employed in producing the commodities consumed by the worker) constitute the surplus value which is gratuitously pocketed by the owner of the means of production in virtue of the fact that he is owner. In this way Marx attains to the qualitative notion of the income of capital, or explains whereof that income effectively consists. It remains to determine the quantity of income, which cannot be specified unless there have previously been precisely determined the measure and the figure of wages.

Now though it be true that the growth of accumulation virtually tends to bring about an increase in the amount paid in wages, it is nevertheless within the power of the capitalist to obviate this undesirable event by investing the growing accumulation in the form of technical capital, which by its very nature is without influence upon wages. But the capitalist can do more than this. He can transform into technical capital a part of the capital which has hitherto been utilised in paying wages, thus throwing some of the workers out of employment, or creating an industrial reserve army. This reserve army, on the one hand stifles all resistance on the part of the workers in active employment, keeping their wages at a level which will purchase the barest necessaries, and on the other hand permits to capitalist industry the sudden expansions in times of prosperity which to the capitalist are so desirable and so profitable. Thus Marx's qualitative investigation is succeeded by a quantitative investigation, so that we learn, not only what surplus value is, but that it is equal to all the excess over and above the more or less limited subsistence of the worker, and that the worker is not merely defrauded of part of the value resulting from his labour, but is reduced to a wretched pittance, happy if he can secure this, and if he be not condemned by the hopeless entanglements of capitalist relationships to submergence in the backwater of the most terrible poverty. The result is that to the favoured recipients of surplus value there is subject a brutalised crowd reduced to a narrow wage, while at a yet lower level there struggles in the morass the amorphous mass of those who are condemned to labour without end.

We thus realise, adds Marx, how profit is born of capital and is in its turn transformed into capital. But none of the considerations hitherto adduced suffice to make it clear what was the origin of primitive capital, that which first of all gave birth to profit, and consequently cannot be the product of profit. The celebrated section on the secret of primitive accumulation was intended to solve this problem. Classical political economy, said Marx, regarded the formation of primitive capital as an episode which occurred during the first days of creation. In times long gone by, there were two sorts of people: one, the diligent, intelligent, and above all frugal élite; the other, lazy rascals, spending their substance, and more, in riotous living. Thus it came to pass before long that the former became impoverished whilst the latter grew wealthy, and the wealthy earned the gratitude of the poor by hiring these to work for them in return for a paltry wage. The theological legend of original sin tells us how man came to be condemned to eat his bread in the sweat of his brow; but the economic history of original sin reveals to us that there are people to whom this is by no means essential. We learn that one section of humanity has succeeded in eluding the divine judgment and in procuring for itself bread and cakes by the sweat of others.

Unfortunately, continues Marx, a conscientious questioning of history discloses that primitive capital originated in very various ways, of a character anything but idyllic. Until the close of the fifteenth century there existed in England a race of peasant proprietors, nominally subject to the jurisdiction of the great lords of the soil. But the increasing demand for wool which resulted from the expansion of the Flemish wool industry, and the increasing demand for flesh meat consequent upon the growth of population, induced the great landowners to destroy an agrarian system by which their returns from rent were rendered practically nil. The free cultivators were brutally evicted from the fields which their ancestors had arduously tilled for centuries past, to be replaced by shepherds and flocks, the crowds of the expropriated hastening to the towns to offer the strength of their arms for hire. Here they happened upon a rout of usurers, traders, house-owners, enriched craftsmen, and lucky speculators; and here too were those who had expropriated them, the landowners who had heaped up savings by fair means or foul, but had hitherto been unable to turn their savings to account owing to the restrictions imposed by the corporative economy (guild system). These accepted as a gift from heaven the influx of the proletarian multitude, and were not slow in setting the new-comers to work on behalf of the growing manufactures. Modern capitalist industry thus originated in a terrible expropriation of the working population which transformed the independent peasants into an impoverished and hunger-stricken mob. But historic nemesis awaits this society conceived in theft, and Marx predicts its disastrous end in the ominous words: " The knell of capitalist property will sound; the expropriators will be expropriated."

The fulfilment of the process will be effected by the forces inherent in the mechanism of the capitalist economy. The more extensive the development of that economy, the fiercer becomes the internecine struggle between the individual aggregations of capital, the more extensive become the accumulations of wealth in the hands of capitalists of the upper stratum, and the smaller becomes the number of these; correlatively there takes place an increase in the size of the working and poverty-stricken crowd, the more hopeless and more pitiful becomes its degradation, whilst simultaneously its cohesion grows more compact, for the workers are disciplined and organised by the very process which associates labour in the factory and upon the land. At a given moment, when the number of mammoth capitalists has conspicuously diminished, and when the pullulating mass of proletarians has increased to an immeasurable degree and has been forced down into the most abject poverty, it will at length be easy to the dispossessed to expropriate the small group of usurpers. Thus the expropriation of the masses by the few, which greeted the dawn of the contemporary economic order, will be counterposed by the expropriation of the restricted number of masters at the hands of the proletarian masses, and this will triumphantly herald a calmer and more resplendent sunrise.

A broad outline has now been given of the marvellous work which, whatever judgment we may feel it necessary to pass upon the value of the doctrines it enunciates, will remain for all time one of the loftiest summits ever climbed by human thought, one of the imperishable monuments of the creative powers of the human mind. Above all we are impressed and charmed by the magnificent quality of the exposition, in which but one defect can be pointed out, and this was probably imposed by the abnormal conditions under which the author wrote. We allude to the last chapter, the one that crowns the story of the historic expropriation of the workers with the eloquent example of the colonies. Logically this chapter should precede the penultimate chapter, wherein Marx, from his account of these terrible happenings, casts the horoscope of revolution. It is probable that the inversion was deliberate, for the prophetic call to the proletarian revolution would have been more likely to attract the attention of the censorship had it been placed at the end of the volume. Apart from this trifling matter, we cannot but admire the shapely pyramidal construction, the harmonious and flowing movement of the book, which, passing from the most subtle disquisitions upon the algebra of value, deals with the complexities of factory life and machine production, plunges into the inferno of workshops and mines and into the infamous stews of unspeakable poverty, to conclude with a description of the tragic expropriation of a suffering population. The work is a masterpiece wherein all is great, all alike incomparable and wonderful—the acuteness of the analysis, the statuesque majesty of the whole, the style vibrant with sorrow or with indignation according as the author is sympathising with the woes of the poor or scourging the villainies of the mighty, the vast learning, and the torrential impetus of passion. There is a stupendous harmony of irreconcilables, so that, as in the mysterious creations of nature, we find an almost inconceivable association of real symmetry with apparent disorder; an association of minute attention to detail with monumental synthesis, an association of mathematics with history, an association of repose with movement; so that in all its fibres the book seems to be the offspring of an unfathomable and transcendental union between superhuman labour and superhuman pain.

Nothing, therefore, is more natural or more readily explicable than the phenomenal success of *Capital*, a success which has rarely been paralleled in the history of intellectual productions. Translated into almost every language (recently even into Chinese); eagerly read by men of learning no less than by statesmen, by reactionaries as well as by rebels; quoted in parliaments and in meetings of the plebs, from the pulpit and from the platform, in huts and in palaces—it speedily secured a world-wide reputation for its author, making him the idol of the most irreconcilable classes and of the most contrasted stocks. Whereas, in fact, the prophetic announcement of the glorious advent of collective property led to the assembling round Marx of all the common people of the west, who hailed him as avenger, as leader, and as seer of the onward march of the proletariat; in such countries as Russia, where capitalist development was as yet in its infancy, the bourgeois

KARL MARX

classes sang the praises of the book which announced the historic mission of capitalism, and thus it was that the idol of the western pétroleurs became in the far east of Europe the fetich of bankers and manufacturers.

After the first shock of surprise, however, readers turned to the dispassionate analysis of the individual doctrines advocated in the work, and were not slow to bring to light certain gaps and sophisms. To say truth, no sovereign importance can be attributed to any of these criticisms, nor is it necessary to make much of the numerous attacks upon the statistical demonstrations of *Capital*. It is undeniable that Marx's thesis of the progressive concentration of wealth into the hands of an ever-diminishing number of owners, and of the correlatively progressive impoverishment of the common people, has not been confirmed. It has indeed been confuted by the most authoritative statistics collected since the publication of the book, for these show that the greater recipients of income increase more than proportionally to the medium and lesser recipients, whereas the number of taxpayers in the lowest grades diminishes, with a proportionate increase in the number of those at a slightly higher level. Further, as far as this last fact is concerned, there can be no doubt that wages have increased of late, so that they not merely rise above the miserable level of bare subsistence specified by Lassalle, but also rise above the level (which is still miserable, though a trifle higher) expressed in the calculations of Marx. It is, however, needful to add that the Marxist thesis merely points to a general tendency, and does not imply a denial that more or less considerable fluctuations may occur at particular periods. Moreover, the concentration of wealth does not find expression solely in the diminution of the numerical proportion between the greater and the lesser recipients of income, but in addition in a diminution of the ratio between the taxpayers and the population and in an increase in the contrast between the wealth of the recipients of income in various grades. Further, the most authoritative statistics demonstrate a growing diminution in the ratio between the owners and the general population. Again, no one can deny that the contrast between high grade and low grade incomes has of late exhibited an enormous increase; that banking concentration and the sway of the banks over industry (a source of increasing disparity in fortunes) has attained in recent years an intensity which even Marx could not have foreseen; and that, subsequently to the publication of *Capital* and to the death of its author, the social fauna has been enriched by an economic animal of a species previously unknown, the multimillionaire, whose existence undeniably reveals an unprecedented advance in capitalist concentration. Nay more, after Marx's death, agrarian and industrial concentration attained preposterous proportions, such as he had never ventured to predict. In the American Union, a single landed estate will embrace territories equal to entire provinces, while industrial capital becomes amassed by milliards in the hands of a few despotic trusts, so that two-thirds of the entire working population are employed by one twentieth of all the separate enterprises in the country. These statements concern the apex of the social pyramid; but even at the base of that structure the phenomena are far from invalidating the Marxist conception to the extent which many contend. Correlatively with the undeniable rise in wages (which, moreover, has been arrested of late, and has been replaced by a definite movement of retrogression), there has occurred an enormously greater increase in income, and therefore a deterioration in the relative condition of the workers. There has further been manifest an increasing instability of employment, so that unemployment has become more widespread and more frequent, exposing the working classes to impoverishment and incurable degradation.

Marx's other theses, however, are open to more serious objection. Retracing the thread of his demonstrations with special attention to his study of primitive accumulation, no one can deny the absolute authenticity of the facts he narrated. Nor can Marx be blamed for having restricted his historic demonstration to England; though in actual fact the expropriation of the cultivators has been carried out everywhere, openly or tacitly, and everywhere this expropriation has been an initial stage in the foundation of capitalist property. Even Russia, who flattered herself upon her independence of the universal law and upon escaping the fated expropriation of her peasants, Russia, whom Marx himself, as if in a sudden fit of mental aberration, was on the point of excluding from the sphere of his generalisations, has to submit to the invariable rule, and to witness the transformation of her independent peasant proprietors into proletarians. The constitutional defect of this portion of Marx's book is of a very different character. Although he tells the story of the expropriation of the cultivators, he fails to explain why such expropriation must always take place, he fails to bring this great historical event beneath the sway of a universal economic theory. Now, putting aside the incongruity that a book essentially founded upon logical demonstration should all at once break off that demonstration to turn to a historical disquisition and a simple record of facts, no one has any right to construct a theoretical generalisation upon the bare narration of hard facts without referring these to the general psychological and logical causes which have produced them. It cannot be denied that in this respect Marx's demonstration presents a defect which it is impossible to make good.

Yet more serious criticism may be directed against the theory of the industrial reserve army, the theory wherein Marx attempts to sum up the law of population of the capitalist era. For the theory is wholly based upon the premise that the conversion of wage capital into technical capital is competent to bring about the permanent unemployment of labour, or definitively to reduce the demand for labour. Now this premise will not hold, for technical capital, by promptly increasing the profit of capital, and by lowering the price of the product in the long run, provides for the capitalist, first of all, and subsequently for the consumer, the possibility of fresh savings, and these in the end create a further demand for labour, so that sooner or later there will be a call upon the active services of the workers who are temporarily unemployed. Vain, therefore, is any attempt to make technical capital responsible for the relative excess of population, which technical capital cannot possibly produce, for this phenomenon must be referred to the presence and to the activity of a very different variety of capital, and one not considered by Marx, namely unproductive capital.

But these criticisms, which after all touch no more than points of detail, are mere trifles in comparison with the incurable contradictions in which the author's fundamental theory is involved. In fact, by a vigorous deduction from his premise that the value of commodities is measured by the mass of labour incorporated in them, Marx arrives at the fundamental and logical distinction between constant capital and variable capital. If, however, the value of products be exclusively determined by the mass of labour incorporated in them, it is evident that the capital invested in machinery or in raw material can only transmit to the product a value exactly equal to the quantity of labour contained therein, without adding any surplus, and that it is therefore constant capital; whereas wage capital transmits to the product value equal to all the quantity of labour which it maintains and sets in motion, a quantity which, as we know, exceeds the quantity of labour contained in the capital itself. In other words, wage capital, besides reproducing its own value, furnishes a supplement or a surplus value, and is therefore variable capital. Consequently surplus value arises exclusively from variable capital, and is therefore precisely proportional to the quantity of this capital. It further ensues that of two undertakings employing equal amounts of aggregate capital, the one which employs a larger proportion of constant capital ought to furnish a profit and a rate of profit lower than that furnished by the other. But free competition among the capitalists enforces an equal rate of profit upon the capitals invested in the various undertakings, and leads to the immediate abandonment of undertakings requiring a greater proportion of constant capital, and to the correlative expansion of the others. There consequently results an increase in the value of the products of the former undertakings, and a diminution in the value of the products of the latter. This process continues until the value of the respective products furnishes an equal rate of profit to the capitals respectively employed in producing them. Value, therefore, though in the first instance it is equivalent to the labour employed in producing the products, necessarily diverges from that standard in the end, and has then an utterly different measure. Thus the theory we are discussing is peremptorily refuted, or is reduced to absurdity.

From the outset Marx is distinctly aware of the existence of this striking contradiction, which emerges in so formidable a manner in the first stage of his investigation; he frankly recognises it, but postpones its solution to the later volumes of his treatise. On the very morrow, indeed, of the publication of the first volume, he ardently set to work once more, and sketched to his friend, in monumental pages, the design of the complete book. Just as St. Augustine was grieved that the duties of his episcopate deprived him of the hours which he would have preferred to devote to the writing of a volume to be the crown of his *City of God*, so Marx was harassed by the thought of the time which the work of party organisation filched from his scientific labours, and it was solely that he might escape from the absorbing engagements involved in the former task that in the Hague congress of 1872 he proposed the transfer of the International to New York. But now we unexpectedly reach a "dead point" in the biography of our thinker, for his mental life, otherwise so normal and so brilliant, here suddenly becomes obscured, and is tinged with mystery and enigma. For, on the one hand, Marx clearly affirmed, and showed by his actions, that he definitely wished to devote himself to the completion of his treatise, whereas, on the other hand, it is undeniable that after the publication of the first volume of *Capital*, he never wrote another line of the book, and that all the posthumous additions to this volume were composed

KARL MARX

prior to 1867. I do not mean to imply that during subsequent years he gave himself up to inertia or repose, for it was during this period that he wrote all the economic section in Engels' booklet against Dühring; he learned Russian; he read the agricultural statistics of numerous countries and the reports on poverty in Ireland; he studied the matriarchal system; carried on ingenious discussions with Engels concerning Carey's theory of rent and Bastiat's theory of the cost of reproduction; threw light on the influence of fluctuations in the value of money upon the rate of profit; sketched a mathematical theory of commercial cycles—in a word, his thought-process remained so active that when a certain publisher asked for the right to issue his complete works, he replied, "My works, those which represent my present thought, are not yet written." But the essential work of his life, the work which had been so much cherished and which he again and again turned over in his thoughts, seems, as far as palpable traces are concerned, to have been entirely dismissed from his mind. We thus look on, marvelling and grieved, at the sight of the enfeebled hero withdrawing from the field, what time his banner, whose staff is not yet firmly implanted in the ground, is left as a target for the easy assaults of his emboldened adversaries.

There certainly contributed to this intellectual shipwreck the illnesses and the misfortunes from which Marx suffered during the later years of his life. His health had been gravely undermined by overwork during the composition of the first volume of *Capital* and during the task of proletarian organisation; trouble from boils alternated with bronchitis, liver disorder, headache, and lumbago. In vain did he seek health in gentler climes, at Ramsgate, Ventnor, Neuenahr, Carlsbad, Algiers, Monte Carlo, Vevey, and other fashionable health resorts. All attempts at cure proving inefficacious, he had at length to settle down once more in London. In 1881 occurred the death of his wife; while the death of his beautiful daughter Jenny, Longuet's wife, in January 1883 was, if possible, a yet more cruel blow. Marx never recovered from this last shock; henceforward he was a broken man, the mere shadow of his former self; he passed his time contemplating the portraits of his two dear ones which Engels was to bury with him, and he no longer took any interest in the world around him or in the social tumult of which he was the inspirer and the originator. He died suddenly at two in the afternoon of March 14, 1883, while seated in his study chair. The titanic brain, which had given a new world to humanity, which had broken once for all the spiritual and material bondage of mankind, had ceased to live and to vibrate.

Most distressing of all, he had taken with him to the grave the solution of the formidable enigma which everyone, the vulgar and the thinkers alike, had expected his genius to solve, and which no one else could unravel. It is true that shortly before his death he showed his friend the bulky manuscripts dictated in earlier days relating to the *Criticism of Political Economy*, suggesting that something might be made of this collection. It is also true that Engels, faithful executor of his divinity's wishes, devoted himself with splendid zeal to the publication of the manuscripts. But alas what delusion was in store for the admirers of the master! What a Russian campaign of disaster organised by enthusiastic lieutenants to the hurt of this Napoleon of thought!

In 1885, two years after the death of Marx, there was published under Engels' supervision a so-called second volume of *Capital*. But the careless and pedestrian editorship, the long theoretical disquisitions making no appeal to facts for their justification, disquisitions in which the argumentative thread is continually broken, suffice to show that what we have before us is not a book, hardly even a sketch for a book, but a series of casual writings composed for the purposes of study and for personal illumination. Moreover, the work is wholly devoted to uninspiring monetary discussions upon the circulation of capital, to dissertations concerning fixed and circulating capital, the formation of metallic reserves, the circulation of commodity-capital, etc. Noteworthy, in any case, are the investigations which aim at throwing light on the process in virtue of which there is effected the formation of metallic reserves which remain out of circulation for a longer or shorter period. If, says Marx, a certain commodity requires for its production six months of labour, and cannot be sold until two months after its production has been completed, the capitalist, if he is to continue the work of production during the period in which the commodity remains unsold, has need of additional capital which he could dispense with if the sale could be effected immediately after production. But when, at the close of the circulation period, the capitalist resumes possession of the capital first utilised and realises it in money, he has no immediate need of all this capital, but only of the quantity necessary to make good the additional capital which he has invested, that is to say, a quantity of capital equal to the difference between the primary capital and the supplementary capital; consequently the excess remains at liberty, and goes to constitute and to increase monetary reserves. These reserves are formed in addition, and by an analogous process, on account of the wear of machinery; for the portions of value transmitted by the machines to the product and correlative to the wear of these machines are pent up until the day of the complete destruction of the machines or of their necessary replacement. Thus the difference between the period of production and the period of exchange of the commodities, and the difference between the period of economic redintegration and the period of technical redintegration of the productive machinery, give rise to the formation of monetary or capitalistic reserves, which become in their turn the source of intricate developments and interesting complications. The book likewise contains a masterly, though wordy and disconnected, account of the circulation of capital. But absolutely nowhere does it touch on or even hint at the theoretical enigma left unsolved in the first volume. Solely in Engels' preface do we find an announcement that the definitive solution will be furnished in a subsequent volume, and a suggestion that in the interim economists engage in a sort of academic debate, and bring forward their respective solutions. There actually took part in this strange competition, with varying success, Conrad Schmidt, Landé, Lexis, Skworzoff, Stiebeling, Julius Wolf, Fireman, Lafargue, Soldi, Coletti, Graziadei, and myself. At length, however, in 1894, appeared the third volume, which was to reveal to an impatient world the desired solution.

The solution reduces itself to this. It is true, says Marx, that the value commensurate to labour ends by assigning to the capitals respectively employed as constant and as variable, different rates of profit, and that this is radically incompatible with competition. But it is likewise true that products are not actually sold for their value, but for their price of production, which is equal to the capital consumed plus profit at the ordinary rate on the total capital employed. Certainly if we consider the mass of products sold, we find that their total price is precisely equal to their total value. But this integral value is not distributed among the various products in proportion to the quantity of labour incorporated in them, but in a lesser or greater proportion, according as the products themselves contain a greater or less proportion of the mean between the constant capital and the total capital; that is to say, the products containing a proportion of constant capital superior to the mean are sold at a price above their value in order to eliminate the deficiency of profit due to the preponderance of the capital which does not produce surplus value; whereas the products containing a proportion of constant capital inferior to the mean are sold at a price less than their value so as to eliminate the excess of profit due to the preponderance of the capital that produces surplus value; whilst only the products containing the mean proportion of constant capital and total capital are sold at a price precisely identical with their value.

But it soon becomes apparent that this so-called solution is little more than a play upon words, or, better expressed, little more than a solemn mystification. For when economists endeavour to throw light upon the laws of value, they naturally consider the value at which the commodities are actually sold, and not a fantastical or transcendental value, not a value which neither possesses nor can possess any concrete relationship to facts. It may well be that value as determined by abstract economic theory will not always correspond precisely with value as a concrete fact, for the complexities and the manifold vicissitiudes of real life impose obstacles; it may well be, indeed, that to the rigidity of normal value, constituting the type of the relationship of exchange, we ought to counterpose the comparatively transient fluctuations of current value. But it must be understood that no logical fact should stand in the way of the realisation of normal value, for this, conversely, ought to be derived by logical necessity from fundamental economic premises. Of a value, indeed, which not only is not realised, but is not logically capable of realisation, the economist neither can nor ought to take any account; he should show in what respect, instead of being the expression of what value is, it is the expression of what value is not and cannot be; he should point out the negation of every correct and positive theory of value. Now this value commensurate to labour, value as defined by Marx's theory, not merely has its realisation restricted or modified by the vicissitudes of reality, but further, as Marx himself is constrained to recognise, it is not logically capable of realisation, seeing that it would give rise to results incompatible with the most elementary advantage of those who effect the exchange of commodities; consequently, it is not merely an abstraction remote from reality, but is incompatible with reality; not only is it an impossibility in the realm of fact, but further and above all it is a logical impossibility. Thus, far from effecting the salvation of the threatened doctrine, this alleged solution administers a death-blow, and implies the categorical negation of what it professes to support. For what meaning can there possibly be in this reduction of value to labour, the doctrine dogmatically affirmed in the first volume, to one who already knows that the author is himself calmly prepared to jettison it? Is there any reason for surprise at Marx's hesitation to publish this so-called defence; need we wonder that his hand trembled, that his spirit quailed, before the inexorable act of destruction?

Despite all, however, genius will not be denied, and even this volume contains here and there masterly disquisitions, enriching the science of economics with new and fertile truths. It will be enough, in this connection, to refer to two theories. The first of these, the theory of the decline in the rate of profit, though not free from objection, is none the less inspired and profound. The second is the theory of absolute rent, a brilliant and acute deduction from the Marxist theory of value. This theory, indeed, as we saw just now, leads to the conclusion that value commensurate to labour furnishes an extra profit to the capital which produces commodities requiring for their production an above-average proportion of variable capital. Now, where free competition exists, such extra profit cannot continue, and must necessarily be eliminated by a reduction in the price of the product to a point below its value. But when competition is not fully free, there is no reason why such extra profit should not be permanent. Now agrarian production requires an abnormally high proportion of variable capital, and consequently agricultural produce, when sold for its value, furnishes an extra profit. But since land is a monopolised element, this extra profit can be permanently assigned to the owners of the soil, because there is no effective competition to prevent their continuing to draw it. There thus comes into existence an absolute land rent, in opposition to or in addition to the differential rent of Ricardo's theory. This absolute rent is not due to the varying cost of production in different areas; it is not the exclusive appanage of lands more favourably situated or of lands of better quality; it arises solely

KARL MARX

from the excess in the value of agrarian produce over its cost of production, and is a general attribute of land per se, in virtue of its quality as a monopolised element. Marx acutely studies the manifold varieties of this rent, according as it is rendered in work, in produce, or in money; and with sound and far-reaching intuition he deduces from his theory explanations of the intricate agrarian relationships among the various peoples of the globe. Nor is this the only gem with which the work is adorned. Very remarkable are the pages upon merchants' capital and money-lenders' capital, on their despotic predominance prior to the inauguration of the capitalist regime, and upon their inevitable dissolution after the advent of that régime. The closing pages, however, seem to breathe a vague weariness, and we find hardly any trace of masterly theoretical discussion of the class struggle, of its origin, of the instruments through which it operates, although this discussion, according to the author's original plan, was to be the monumental crown of the titanic work.

Thus, however fragmentarily, and thanks to the help of lieutenants and of disciples who were not always adequately instructed, the theoretical treatise, at once the pride and the torment of our prophet, at length arrived at completion. But the reader will not forget that to the positive treatment of his subject, Marx always counterposed a historico-critical investigation of the theories of his precursors, and in the more mature design of his work such an exposition was to follow upon the exposition of his own doctrines and to form their apt complement. It remained, therefore, to bring to light this last part of his researches, a duty which was faithfully discharged (after the death of Engels), by Karl Kautsky, with the publication of the *History of*

KARL MARX

the Theory of Surplus Value, which appeared in four volumes during the years 1905 to 1910. Substantially, though publishers have preferred to treat it as a work apart, this book is nothing other than the concluding section of *Capital*, announced in the preface to the first volume, where the author tells of a sequel to be devoted to the history of this theory. In the posthumous work Marx traces the development of the theory of surplus value through its three essential stages, the prericardian, the Ricardian, and the postricardian. To the first of these phases belong the theories of the physiocratic school, whose essence Marx grasps with marvellous acuteness, maintaining that the theories in question were the doctrinal reflection of the interests of the rising capitalist class, constrained to pretend that its own economic claims were the logical expression of the advantage of the landed and feudalist classes then politically dominant. Particularly noteworthy are the comments on the teaching of Adam Smith. The second volume contains a searching criticism of the Ricardian system, and above all of Ricardo's theories of value and of profit. In the third section Marx passes judgment on the theories of Ricardo's successors, Malthus, Senior, and John Stuart Mill, for these writers, says Marx, follow the setting sun of bourgeois economic science, follow that science to its now inevitable doom. It was a fixed idea with Marx that the theoretical analysis of capitalist relationships had secured its fullest and most adequate expression in the pages of Ricardo; he believed that Ricardo had supplied the ultimate synthesis possible on these lines; that any further progress of economic science in its bourgeois trappings had become impossible; that its decline amid contradictions and perversions was inevitable; and that economics could only be renewed and reborn when the disintegrated vesture of bourgeois economic relationships had been completely thrown aside to give place to a definitive and superior social form. It is scarcely necessary to point to the sophisms and the arbitrary assumptions upon which this concept is based; but it must be admitted that the poverty, deficiency, and incurable vanity of current economic science increasingly tend to give the theory an awkward semblance of truth.

To-day, now that the fruits of Marx's meditations, be it only as the result of the work of collaborators, be it only with many gaps and imperfections, have all been given forth to the reading world, it is at length possible to take a general view, and to pass a dispassionate judgment upon the pre-eminent worth of his writings. The most austere criticism must bow reverently before such gigantic mental attainments as have few counterparts in the history of scientific thought, garnering from all branches of knowledge on behalf of the undying cause of mankind. The most inexorable criticism should recognise in Marx the supreme merit of having been the first to introduce the evolutionary concept into the domain of sociology, the first to introduce it in the only form appropriate to social phenomena and social institutions; not as the unceasing and gradual upward-movement outlined by Spencer, but as the succession of agelong cycles rhythmically interrupted by revolutionary explosions, proceeding in accordance with the manner sketched by Lyell for geological evolution, and in our own time by de Vries for biological evolution. With the aid of this concept, strictly positive and scientific, Marx triumphantly overthrew, on the one hand classical economic science, taken prisoner by its own notion of a petrified society, and on the other the philosophy of law and idealist socialism which were convinced that it was possible to mould the world in accordance with the arbitrary conceptions of the thinker. Looked at in this light, the work of Marx presents a new instrument for the use of the philosophy of history and for the use of sociology; and it has contributed no less powerfully to the advance of technological science, thanks to the writer's masterly investigation into the successive forms of the technical instrument of productive machinery. In this respect more than in any others Marx may be compared with Darwin, and may indeed be spoken of as the Darwin of technology: for no one has ever had a profounder knowledge than Marx of the structural development of the industrial mechanism, no one else has followed step by step the formation and upward elaboration of productive technique; just as Darwin, with invincible mental energy, traced the evolution of animal technique, the development of the functional apparatus of organised beings. This physiology of industry, which is now the least studied and least appreciated of Marx's scientific labours, nevertheless constitutes his most considerable and most enduring contribution to science. Noteworthy, in especial, and destined to form a permanent and integral part of the economic science of the world, are Marx's analyses of money, credit, the circulation of capital, poverty, primitive accumulation, not to speak of the historico-critical investigations into the work of the British classical economists—for here Marx, without prejudice to the merits of those who have fought honourably in this difficult arena, will ever remain the most brilliant and most profound commentator. For these mighty and noble contributions, his name will be inscribed in imperishable letters in the history of creative thought.

But if his sociological, historical, and technological investigations, if his studies of money, the banking system, and industrial statistics, be so many intellectual jewels of which no praise can be excessive, it is none the less true that his fundamental economic theory is essentially vitiated and sophistical, and that he is himself responsible for reducing it to hopeless absurdity. We arrive, therefore, at this remarkable result: that Marx, whose primary aim it was to be a theorist of political economy, and to deal only in subsidiary fashion with the philosophy of history and of technology, secured a triumphant success in these subordinate fields; whereas in respect of the fundamental object of his thought, his work was a complete failure.

Nor can we deny that the very design of Marx's work, however marvellous in the Michelangelesque grandeur of its ensemble, does not satisfy those who insist upon strictly scientific method, and that in this respect Marx stands far below the great masters of positive science. For, however admirable and however great this man who succeeded in subsuming an entire world within the limits of an extremely simple initial principle, and whose life was but the development of an equation which he had formulated at its outset, how far more straightforward and trustworthy, how far more scientific, was the method of Darwin, who never formulated any apriorist principles, but, quite free from preconceptions, accepted phenomena in the order of progressive complexity in which life itself presented them. Darwin first studied the natural formation of organised beings, then devoted himself to an examination of the larger types, and was finally led to infer their development by evolutionary growth. This method, which follows nature and reflects it, seems far more worthy of respect, far more honest, far more strictly scientific, than the other method, which manipulates the truth, does violence to the truth, in order to accommodate it to hidden ends.

There is no reason, therefore, to be surprised that such a flood of criticism should have been directed against this colossus, or that on the morrow of the completion of Marx's work the skies of the two hemispheres should have rung with disorderly clamour proclaiming the crisis, nay the failure, of Marxism. But that which is less easy to understand, that which discloses the utter immaturity of economic science as well as of contemporary socialism, is that criticism has not been directed against the truly vulnerable point of the system, but has been solely concerned in attacking its better defended and less fragile parts. In fact, the scientific and socialist currents partially or wholly opposed to Marxism display a strange reverence for his theory of value, or do not venture to attack it, but concentrate their forces against the statistical and historical theories which are the deductions and complements of the Marxist theory of value. In this respect the critics of Marxism form two very distinct groups. The first of these, the reformist or revisionist school, has a high respect for the master's theory of value, and reiterates it as an indisputable truth; whereas reformists criticise the theory of increasing misery, the theory of the concentration of capital, and above all the catastrophic vision of the proletarian revolution. The writers of this school affirm, and think that in so doing they are setting up an antithesis to Marxism, that to await the millennium of the social revolution is futile utopianism; they contend, that the progressive reduction in the number of the wealthy, paralleled by the ceaseless increase in the number of more and more impoverished proletarians, a development which according to Marx's vision was to provide the apparatus destined to destroy the contemporary economy, is negatived by an actual tendency towards a more democratic distribution of commodities; and they insist, therefore, that socialism should aim at securing the triumph of its cause by means that are less violent but far more efficacious, namely by social legislation or by reforms tending to reduce inequality. Now, without troubling to repeat what I have already said, that the Marxist dynamic of the distribution of wealth is far from being as completely negatived by contemporary facts as these critics are pleased to insist, I merely propose to point out that this paying of high honour to reform and social legislation nowise conflicts with the doctrine or with the work of Marx, who, on the contrary, was the first to throw into high relief the pre-eminent value of social legislation, devoting classical chapters to the elucidation of its most memorable manifestations. In this light, therefore, revisionism or reformism, far from being a negation or correction of Marxism, is a specific application or partial realisation of the doctrine, for it brings into the lime-light one of the numerous sides of that marvellous polyhedron, and deserves credit for having explained and developed this particular aspect of Marxism. But revisionism errs gravely in that it wishes to replace the beautiful and complex multiplicity of the Marxist system by forcing us to contemplate this unilateral aspect alone. The reformists err in that they fail to see that legislative reforms, though desirable and extremely opportune, are invariably circumscribed by the prepotent opposition of the privileged classes, and can never do anything more than mitigate a few of the grosser harshnesses of the present system—whilst, precisely because they effect this mitigation, reforms tend to preserve an increasingly unstable economic order from the imminent disaster of a destructive cataclysm.

If the reformist school mutilates Marxism thus violently, by reducing the whole of *Capital* to the paragraphs extolling social legislation, the syndicalists inflict a yet cruder mutilation on the Marxist system by tearing a single page out of *Capital*, to make of this page the alpha and the omega of their revolutionary creed. It is true that Marx, in the thirty-first chapter of *Capital*, makes an explicit appeal to force, the midwife of every old society pregnant with a new one; but this appeal is not made until it has been fully demonstrated that the social revolution can only be effected at the close of a slow and lengthy evolutionary process which shall have caused complete disintegration of the existing economic order and shall have paved the way for its inevitable transformation into a superior order. Now the syndicalists unhesitatingly sponge all this demonstration from the slate, and affirm that the proletarian masses can undertake action at any moment, can violently overthrow the prevailing economic order whenever it shall please them to do so; and they declare that it is needless for revolutionists to keep their eyes fixed upon the clock of history, in order to see if this is about to sound the knell of the present social order. It would be superfluous to demonstrate the absurdity of such a thesis, for the very school which proclaims it has assumed the task of giving it the lie in clamorous accents. For if, as the new apostles of force contend, the proletarian masses can at any moment annihilate the prevailing economic order, why do they not rise against the capitalism they detest, and replace it with the co-operative commonwealth for which they long? Why is it that after so much noisy organisation, after so much declamation and delirious excitement, the utmost they are able to do is to tear up a few yards of railway track or to smash a street lamp? Do we not find here an irrefragable demonstration that force is not realisable at any given moment, but only in the historic hour when evolution shall have prepared the inevitable fall of the dominant economic system?

Thus whatever they can do, it always seems that the infirm will of the disciples who demand an arbitrary renovation of the social system (whether by legal measures or by force) breaks vainly against the fatality of evolution, and that reformism and syndicalism are merely caricatures, counterfeits, or exaggerations of the many-sided and well-balanced theory of the master, who proposed a threefold line of advance: by social legislation; by the activity of the organised workers; and by revolution. In face of these various forms of neo-marxism, the outcome of mutilations and of one-sided exclusivism, Marx redivivus would have excellent reason for repeating his own adage, so thoughtful and so true, " I am not a Marxist." However striking the temporary success of these new forms among the crowd or among the learned, we may confidently predict that neither reformism nor syndicalism will definitively supplant the Marxist system, which despite all and against all remains and will remain a supreme and invincible force at once of theory and of organisation for the proletarian assault upon the long-enduring fortress of property.

The value of Marx's work is, in fact, displayed in the most brilliant light by the detailed criticism of the theorists and by the contrast with opposing trends; all the more when we compare the aspect of economic thought and of proletarian organisation before and after the publication of *Capital*. For if we study the utterances of thinkers upon these matters during the middle of the nineteenth century, we find that nearly all are dominated by the categorical idea that the social order is of an absolutely immobile character, and that none but a few utopians entertain the thought of changing that order by means of precipitate legislation inspired by their individual preconceptions. In any case, it was an idea common to all, to revolutionists as well as to conservatives, that the poverty of the masses was a negative and distressing residue from the economic system, that it was a purely passive feature of that system which must be accepted with resignation, for it could not exercise any propulsive influence in the general social movement. This is substantially the notion which emerges from Victor Hugo's *Les Misérables*, for poverty is here regarded as an overwhelming mass of suffering for which it is impossible to assign the responsibility; it is looked upon as a load pressing with inexorable cruelty upon suffering humanity, which is unable to respond by anything more effective than complaints and tears. But how utterly different is the notion prevailing in our own days upon this matter. Not only is the conviction now rooted in the mind of every thinker that the economic order is subject to unceasing change, is advancing towards predestined destruction; but it is considered certain that the artificer, the demiurge, the most potent factor of this destruction, will be the active resistance, the unrest, the rebellion, of the proletarians in the grasp of the capitalist machine and eager to destroy it. This conception of the dynamogenic function of poverty is the most characteristic feature of the social thought of our day, the feature wherein that thought contrasts most categorically with the ideas of an earlier age. Just as the Christian sect, represented by Gibbon as a mere pathological efflorescence growing on the margin of Roman society, is by the better equipped science of our own time looked upon as having been the most potent solvent of the imperial complex and as the ferment generating a new and better life, so the proletarian masses, regarded by the science and the art of the past as a crushed and pitiful appendage of the bourgeois economy, now appear to contemporary science as the most vigorous among the forces tending to disintegrate that economy, as tending irresistibly to create a higher and better balanced form of association. Correlatively with this development, whereas the proletarians of other days were content to sulk in their hovels as they contemplated the brilliant gyrations of the capitalist constellation, merely cursing in secret the sorrows of their lot, to-day the workers of the two worlds are advancing in serried ranks to the conquest of a new humanity and a new life. Thus the immobility of our fathers has given place to rapid movement; their discouragement and resignation, to rebellious demands; and whereas of old a chasm yawned between the scattered visionaries who entertained dreams of social rebirth and the inert mass of the poverty-stricken, we find to-day that the impoverished are themselves becoming the artificers, the heralds, the pioneers, of the irresistible ascent of humanity towards a juster and better social order. Now all this new moral and social world, unknown to our grandparents, the glory and the plague of science, of society, of contemporary life; all this gigantic tumult of ideas, facts, claims, of assaults, wounds, innovating reconstructions; all this marvellous necromancy is the work of one man, a sage and a martyr. All this we owe to Karl Marx, It measures, concretes, and materialises for us his colossal worth and the omnipotent vastness of his achievement. Though science may well and with full right complain of the gaps in his doctrinal system, though life may furnish the most definite refutations of his theoretical visions, and though future history may display forms of which he never dreamed, nevertheless, no one will ever be able to unseat him from his throne, or to dispute the sovereignty which accrues to him on account of his splendid contributions to civil progress. Whether praised and accepted, or despised and rejected, by practice or by theory, by history or by reason, he will always remain the emperor in the realm of mind, the Prometheus foredestined to lead the human race towards the brilliant goal which awaits it in a future not perhaps immeasurably remote.

For the day is coming. And in that day, when remorseless time shall have destroyed the statues of the saints and of the warriors, renascent humanity will raise in honour of the author of this work of destruction, upon the shores of his native stream, a huge mausoleum representing the proletarian breaking his chains and entering upon an era of conscious and glorious freedom. Thither will come the regenerated peoples bearing garlands of remembrance and of gratitude to lay upon the shrine of the great thinker, who, amid sufferings, humiliations, and numberless privations, fought unceasingly for the ransom of mankind. And the mothers, as they show to their children the suffering and suggestive figure, will say, their voices trembling with emotion and joy: See from what darkness our light has come forth; see how many tears have watered the seeds of our joy; look, and pay reverence to him who struggled, who suffered, who died for the Supreme Redemption.